NORTHABOUT

Sailing the North East and North West Passages

Kneeling at the Last Wave

Up there on the stony shore of the North West Passage
you might discover tears in a man's eyes;
you might discover even a grimace of compassion;
even the undertone of a premonition of affection.

Seafarer, these are my bones
and here is lichen on my skull:
crimson-scabbed, beige-intaglio'd lichen on my skull.
The different shall inherit the earth, if there are any different left.

Paul Durcan

NORTHABOUT

Sailing the North East and North West Passages

JARLATH CUNNANE

The Collins Press

Published in 2006 by

The Collins Press

West Link Park
Doughcloyne
Wilton
Cork

British Library Cataloguing in Publication Data

Cunnane, Jarlath
    Northabout : sailing the North West & North East Passages
    1. North East Passage - Description and travel
    2. North West Passage - Description and travel
    I. Title
    910.9'1632

    ISBN-10: 1905172230
    ISBN-13: 978-1905172238

Book design and typesetting: Anú Design, Tara
Font: Sabon 10.5 point
Printed in Ireland by ColourBooks Ltd.

CONTENTS

ACKNOWLEDGEMENTS

This entire project would never have taken place without the determination and organisational skills of our expedition leader, Paddy Barry. It was he who undertook the daunting task of organising the necessary permissions and permits required for an expedition in polar regions. Not only did he inspire the team members to go that extra mile but, by his enthusiasm, he brought out the best in everybody.

Thanks to all the contributors to this book – Paddy Barry, Frank Nugent, Kevin Cronin, Michael Brogan, Terry Irvine, Rory Casey, John Murray, Brendan Minish – and to Gary Finnegan and all the team members for their photographs. Thanks also to Shay Fennelly for his photographs of our departure. And to Paul Durcan, a special thanks for his poem.

I am told that a sigh of relief was heard from many people in County Mayo when Northabout left Westport in June 2001. At last they could get back to their normal lives again. To the many friends who helped with the building of Northabout, thank you. Some of those whose goodwill was put to the test during the building, include: Liam Canavan, Louis Purton, John Beirne, Padraic Sloyan, Brian Egan, Francois Voignier, Udo Hertfelter, Frank Guilfoyle, Seamus, Frank, Vinnie, and Brendan Salmon, Mick Kelly, Damian Lyons, Eugene O'Malley, Mike Bourke, James Cahill, Eddie Horan, Peter Gargan and Brendan Glavey.

We could never have undertaken this adventure without the support and the understanding of our families during our long absences from home; they had the additional burden of managing our affairs and looking after our interests. We thank you!

I acknowledge with gratitude the support of our major sponsors for their financial assistance: Volvo Cars Ireland, Permanent TSB Bank and Dromoland Castle Hotel. Many other companies and individuals made generous financial contributions or donations of supplies. A special word of thanks to the Arctic enthusiasts who attended our fundraising slide shows throughout the country. We are grateful to our fellow members of the Irish Cruising Club, who supported our efforts and acknowledged our achievements by awarding us the Fastnet Award.

Thanks also to all the team members who stood their watches no matter how difficult the conditions. All played their part, and demonstrated their special skills. I concur with the remark I heard on a cold Siberian night: 'Lesser men couldn't have done it!' To my friends Tom Moran, who kept the machinery working, and Brendan Minish, who installed the radio equipment on board and built the giant directional antenna in his garden to maintain our link with the outside world, a special thanks.

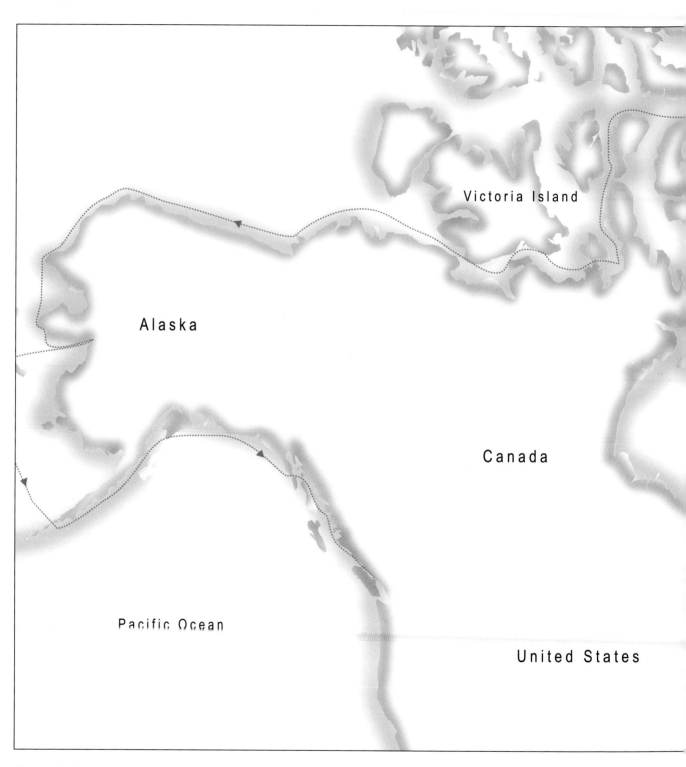

The North West Passage.

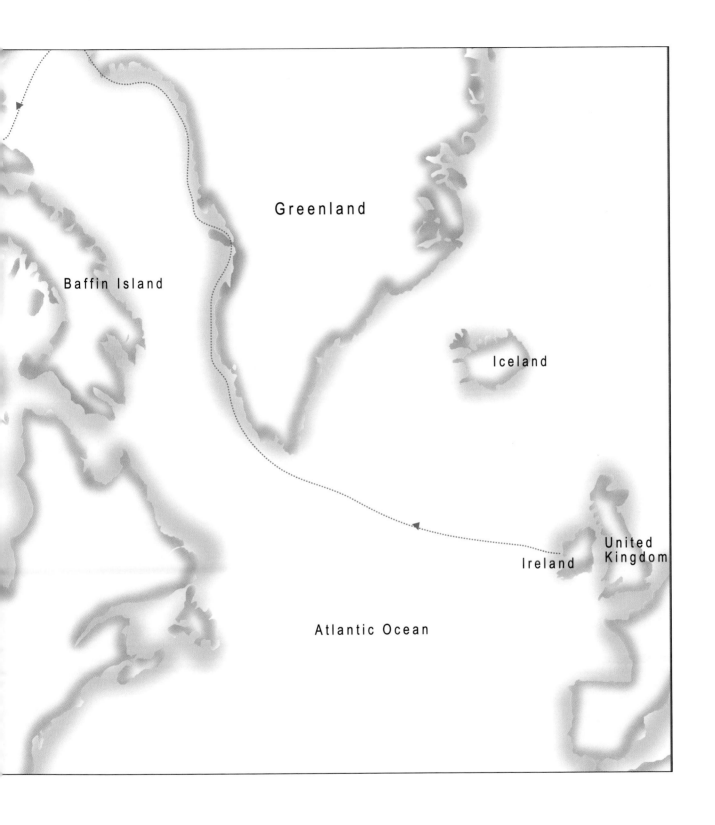

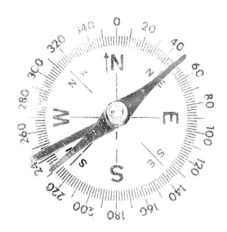

1

FROM PLANS TO LAUNCH

My sailing career began in sailing dinghies, mainly home built. Over the years the boats increased in size. An Atlantic crossing on a friend's yacht in 1986 gave me a taste of the joys of ocean sailing. The result of this delightful new experience was that I built my steel 34-foot sailing cruiser, designed by Van de Stadt, which I called *Lir. Lir's* shakedown cruise was to the Azores in 1990, giving me the confidence to spend the following two seasons cruising the eastern Mediterranean.

My sailing experience was expanding as I learned the moods of the sea.

In 1997 when I was invited to join an expedition to recreate Shackleton's escape from Antarctica, I found that like Shackleton and others I had become utterly obsessed by the beauty of the icy wastes. So it was no great surprise to my friends when they found that my next expedition was to be to northern polar regions.

Like many of our great plans, the decision to sail the North West Passage emerged during a get-together in a Dublin pub, The Cobblestone, in the Smithfield market area.

Paddy Barry and I were old friends and we both worked in the civil engineering industry. Occasionally we met to have a couple of pints and listen to the impromptu music sessions for which The Cobblestone is renowned.

Shackleton's men launching the James Caird *on Elephant Island in April 1916; we set sail in the* Tom Crean *from the same desolate shore in January 1997. (Courtesy SPRI)*

On this occasion Frank Nugent joined us. Frank is an experienced expedition man and climber, with years of experience climbing in the Alps and the Himalayas including Everest. Though his primary interests were in mountaineering, he had sailed with Paddy and I to Scotland for a climbing holiday on Skye, and also sailed with us in Antarctica. That night Frank sang 'The Ballad of Lord Franklin'. It told the story of Lord Franklin's ill-fated expedition in search of the North West Passage in 1847. Maybe this was the inspiration? As the night progressed, the talk swung around to planning a sailing trip to Hudson Bay or another Arctic site.

This would not be our first polar expedition; we had already sailed in the Antarctic in a recreation of Shackleton's small boat journey in 1997 which we called *South-Aris*.

Shackleton's escape from the Antarctic ice by small boat is one of the epic survival journeys in the history of polar exploration. When his ship, the *Endurance*, sank after being crushed by ice in the Weddell Sea, Shackleton and his crew of 27 men managed to salvage three lifeboats from the shipwreck. Across the ice and open sea they made their way to the relative safety of remote and uninhabited Elephant Island. Knowing that there was no prospect of whalers or other shipping coming to rescue them from that rocky, snow-covered island, Shackleton, with five crew sailed for help in the largest of the lifeboats, the *James Caird*, named in honour of the expedition's sponsor.

Sir Ernest Shackleton, the explorer. (Courtesy Royal Geographical Society)

Tom Crean, the strong man of the Scott and Shackleton South Pole expeditions. (Courtesy Scott Polar Research Institute)

Their rescue attempt took them 800 miles to the whaling station in South Georgia across the most windswept ocean in the world. Having reached South Georgia, they landed in King Hakken Bay on the south-west coast. On the other side of the island was the whaling station at Stromness. Because the crew was now exhausted and the boat damaged, Shackleton, with Worsley, the captain, and Irishman Tom Crean, trekked across the mountains and glaciers, reaching the astonished whalers in Stromness after a trek of 36 hours.

Every member of the crew was eventually rescued from Elephant Island through the efforts of Shackleton and his men. Tom Crean, in his lifetime, never received the recognition he deserved for the huge part he played in this epic journey.

We initiated the *South Arís* expedition primarily to try to create public awareness of the part played by Tom Crean in both Scott's and Shackleton's South Pole expeditions. Crean's exploits are now well known and are even commemorated in a Guinness advertisement and an award-winning play.

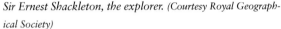

In our South *Arís* expedition 1997, Paddy, Frank and I, with much assistance from others, built a replica of the *James Caird*, which we named *Tom Crean* in memory of our unsung hero.

The *Tom Crean* was shipped from Ireland in a container to the Argentinean port of Ushuia, in Tierra del Fuego, and from there it was transported to King George Island in Antarctica by an ice-breaker.

Tom Crean *on her first sail, before adding ballast.*

There, we were reunited with the *Tom Crean,* having arrived on our chartered support vessel, *Pelagic,* some days previously. The other crew members were Jamie Young (who runs an adventure training school), Mike Barry (a mountaineer), Mick O'Rourke (a cameraman who was making a film of the voyage) and John Bourke (another mountaineer). John also looked after our fundraising and finance.

An overnight sail took us from King George Island to Elephant Island, that isolated rock, the departure point of Shackleton's boat journey. We spent the day on the spit where Shackleton's crew lived under the upturned boats for 148 days. A more desolate place could not be imagined, with no shelter and snow-covered mountains all around. In the evening we followed in Shackleton's wake, bound towards South Georgia. *Tom Crean's* bow broke through the newly-formed sea ice with a tinkling sound as we raised sail. All went well with us for the first 400 miles. The crew adapted to the cold, cramped conditions on board. At this rate of progress we felt another week would see us in South Georgia. It was not to be. Storm force winds on the eighth night created huge breaking seas. The first capsize occurred in the evening. As we lay to a sea anchor listening to the shrieking of the wind, out of nowhere a breaking sea rolled *Tom Crean* completely over. Fortunately, no one was swept overboard, and after what seemed an interminably long time, another sea righted her again.

Tom Crean *on sea trials.*

Top: *The snow-capped mountains of South Georgia which Shackleton crossed on his route from King Haaken Bay to the whaling station at Stromness.*
Right: *King penguins, with a fur seal lying behind them, strut amongst the scrap metal abandoned by the Norwegian whalers in the 1930s.*

While we were upside down I felt we were descending rapidly into the sea's depths, and I feared no one would ever know our fate.

Remarkably little damage was incurred in the capsize, though our spare clothes were swimming amidst tins of food, sleeping bags, broken mugs and gas canisters. After pumping out the water and drying off as best we could, we reported the event to *Pelagic*, our support vessel, which was then about 11 miles downwind.

Pelagic too was having difficulties coping with the seas, despite it being a well-found 57- foot vessel. We asked *Pelagic* to get us a weather forecast.

When they reported back, the forecast was not encouraging; further gales to follow for the next ten days. Twice during the next night we were rolled over again. By now everyone was cold and wet and, after a discussion, in view of the weather prospects, we reluctantly decided to abandon the voyage. We asked *Pelagic* to pick us up. In the morning *Pelagic* came into view, and during a lull in the storm we abandoned *Tom Crean*. I was the last to leave, and with much regret I had to drill a hole in the hull to let her sink. This was a sad event for me. My team of boat builders and I had taken great care in the construction of this fine vessel. But if left afloat it would have been a danger to shipping.

Later we landed in King Hakken Bay, South Georgia, where Shackleton had landed in 1916. Our team re-enacted Shackleton's brave achievement in crossing the island in 36 hours by successfully crossing the mountains of South Georgia to the whaling station at Stromness. This voyage and arduous climb had greatly increased our admiration for Shackleton and his men.

The human mind is remarkable; memories of hardship are soon forgotten. The rigours of participating in our Antarctic adventure had mellowed sufficiently by the year 2000.

The call of the wild again was strong. We began to itch for a new adventure.

✦✦✦

We sat in The Cobblestone discussing various cruising grounds. The obvious options, such as the Mediterranean, were dismissed as too hot, too expensive and too ordinary. Hudson Bay in Canada got a good airing. It promised all the ingredients for a good summer cruise – it was reasonably within reach, it could be completed within an extended annual holiday, promised good sailing and perhaps some mountain climbing. But yet, for all its attractions, Hudson Bay did not entirely appeal to me. I was thinking about the North West Passage. This route, with its reputation of impenetrability, had intrigued me and appealed to me for many years.

The adventurous spirit of the first explorers, and the myths and lore of the North West Passage all gathered in my mind as I listened to the imagery of Frank's song. We had talked of the North West Passage in general terms many times in the past. But now as the evening progressed, we were talking about it more earnestly than ever before. But was a transit of the legendary Northwest Passage possible? We were determined to find out.

A deadline of 1 March 2000 was set for the final decision on whether we would go or not. In the meantime we were each to investigate various aspects of the proposed trip.

Paddy would research the information available about the ice, what permits were required and what logistical difficulties might be involved. Frank would study the history of the discovery of the North West Passage, and I would assess the best type of boat for the voyage.

✦✦✦

Why the Arctic? People often ask why a group of ordinary sailors from Ireland would want to sail the frozen wastes of the Arctic. To this question there is no easy answer.

For me, the attraction lay in seeing the pristine snow-covered landscape, in visiting remote areas seldom seen by man, and in meeting the people who carved out an existence in those inhospitable regions.

We knew the challenges we had to overcome. Our venture was totally unlike some expeditions that were organised as money-making ventures. None of our team could be described as wealthy; all had ordinary jobs and families to look after. The common bond was that we were all friends, all loved sailing, and all loved the wilderness and the beauty of the far north.

Living in Ireland our knowledge of ice was very limited. We never see the sea frozen in our home waters. We had, however, our Antarctic experience, and Paddy had sailed his traditional gaff-rigged Galway Hooker to Greenland and Spitzbergen. So we felt we had a good inkling of the conditions likely to be encountered. We knew the polar ice breaks up for a short time in mid-August before freezing again in September. With such a short season we realised it was necessary to have a strong crew to push on at every opportunity. We would need to have a vessel strong enough to withstand slamming into ice, and the possibility of being frozen in and maybe squeezed by pressure ice. It would be a requirement to carry sufficient food supplies for two seasons and enough fuel to motor at least 1,000 miles. On the plus side we were going to have 24-hour daylight, at least initially, and the Arctic high-pressure zone, which normally develops during the summer, would give us calm, sunny weather – we hoped.

As we all set about our research tasks, excitement about the trip's possibilities began to take hold. Somehow, in the midst of investigating *if* we would do this, the focus shifted to *how* we would do this.

At our next meeting in early January 2000 the plan started to take shape. Since the last meeting I had been in correspondence with another Arctic enthusiast, Terry Irvine from Belfast. Terry had been bitten by the Arctic bug on his previous trip to Greenland on Paddy's Galway hooker, *St Patrick*. I knew Terry had amassed a lot of information on polar boats, and was interested in building a metal boat. We had talked at length about the merits of various designs.

It became apparent that neither my 34-foot steel sloop nor Paddy's wooden hooker was suitable for a long polar voyage. The only solution, given our limited budget, was to build a new boat ourselves.

The search then began for a suitable design. After much discussion on the pros and cons of designs available we concluded the Nadja 15 best met our requirements, as it was specifically designed for polar expeditions.

With Terry also on the project, we decided to go ahead and build. As with all good building projects, the completion date was set: departure on 23 June 2001. Other things might change but this date was firm.

Paddy would be the project leader, and organise delivery of boat-building materials. Frank got the job of organising a brochure for a fund-raising drive, targeting specific potential sponsors. Frank

The crew for the North West Passage at Upernavik, Greenland. Note the hill in the background levelled to form the new airport. Left to right: Kevin Cronin, Michael Brogan, Jarlath Cunnane, Frank Nugent, Paddy Barry, John Murray, Gearóid O'Riain and Terry Irvine.

would also identify areas of interest on the route. My task was to build the boat and be skipper. I would own the boat and invest the proceeds of the sale of my yacht *Lir* in the new boat. Terry would have some of the boat fittings fabricated in Belfast.

With the project now underway, the team was assembled over the next few weeks, each bringing his own particular skill. All were sailors, and were known to one another and most had sailed together. The initial team comprised:

Paddy Barry, project leader, navigator and general organiser
Jarlath Cunnane, skipper and boat builder
Frank Nugent, mountain climber, author, and Arctic historian

Terry Irvine, sailor and Arctic enthusiast
Michael Brogan, ship's doctor, cook and fiddle-player
Kevin Cronin, accountant, pacifier and financial controller
John Coyle, fund-raising
Gearóid O'Riain, electronics and information technology
John Murray, sailor and film-maker
Pat Colleran, radio operator
Brendan Minish, home base radio operator

Sadly Pat lost his battle against cancer before we got underway. His loss was a terrible blow to us all, so suddenly taken from his wife and young family.

John Coyle had to withdraw from sailing because of business commitments and the added burden of the chairmanship of the Galway Races Committee. John, however, did continue to support us in every way possible.

With an initial contribution of £350 from each of the crew, the boat building started.

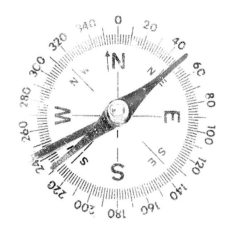

2

THE BOAT

The boat we selected for the adventure was a Nadja 15 designed by Gilbert Caroff of Caroff
–Dufloss Naval Architects, Paris. The Nadja class is one of three expedition boats designed by
Caroff that have all made major polar voyages. Eric Brossier has a modified Super Disco called
Vagabond; and Henk de Velde has an Angelina named *Campina* which will feature later in our
story. The name for our vessel, *Northabout*, was chosen by Mary Barry, Paddy's wife, as it
describes our route, and was also the whalers' name for the route north by Melville Bay,
Greenland.

A brief description of *Northabout:*

- ✦ Length overall 15 metres (49 foot 3ins)
- ✦ Beam 4.4 metres (14 foot 5 ins)
- ✦ Draft minimum (with centreboard raised) 1.4 metres (4 foot 6 ins)
- ✦ Draft maximum (centreboard down) 3 metres (10 foot)

- ✦ 90 HP Perkins Diesel Motor
- ✦ Cooking and heating is by Dickinson Atlantic diesel stove
- ✦ Engine is keel cooled to prevent engine damage while motoring in shallow water when a conventional cooling system might be blocked by dirt or ice
- ✦ Sail area is 185 square metres, (1900 square feet). Northabout is cutter rigged, that is with a mainsail and two headsails set before the mast. The headsails are easily reefed in heavy weather with their roller furling gear
- ✦ Diesel capacity – five tanks containing a total of 1850 litres, giving a range under power of 2000 miles

An expedition to Arctic regions must be self-sufficient. There are few rescue services available, and those that are may be a great distance away. Spare parts may not be available. Therefore, the vessel and equipment must be in first-class order and the crew must possess all the skills required to deal with any breakdown or problem that might arise. For this reason, each member of our crew was chosen for the particular skill they majored in. I always say one can't be good at everything!

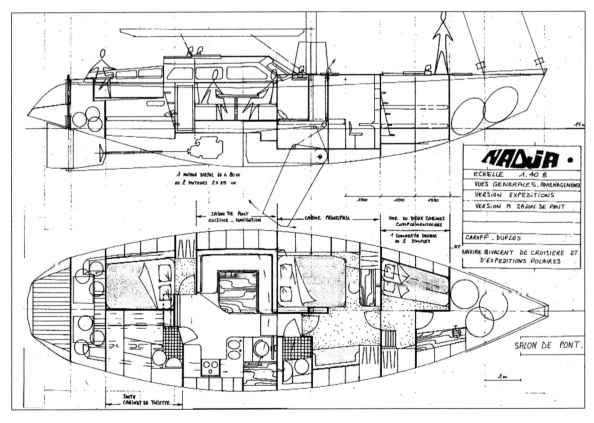

Line drawing of Northabout: *accommodation layout, two single aft cabins were built instead of the double as shown on the drawing. These cabins were occupied by the skipper and the navigator, Jarlath in port cabin and Paddy in starboard cabin.*

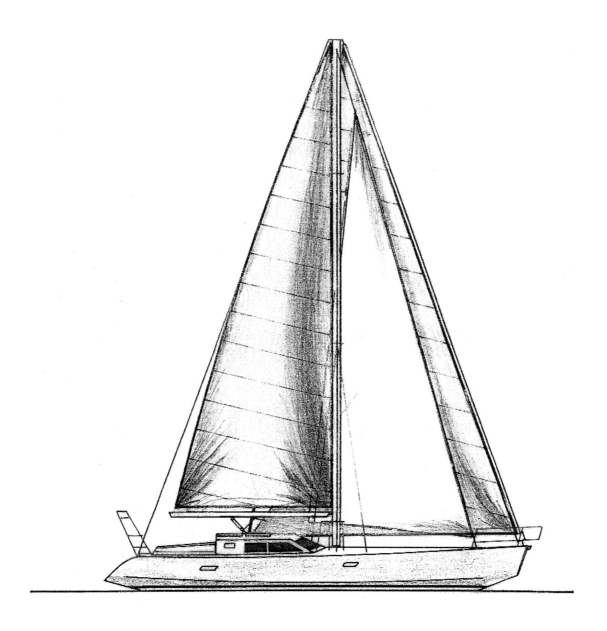

GENOIS SUR ENROULEUR · 88.5 m²
FOC DE SECOURS SUR ETAI LARGABLE 48.5
GRAND VOILE A ENROULEMENT 51.5
ROND DE CHUTE ET LATTES SELON TYPE
D'ENROULEMENT CHOISI POUR LA GRAND
VOILE DANS LE MAT OU DANS LA BOME.

NAJA○

VOILURE SLOOP

BUREAU D'ETUDE CAROFF-DUFLOS

Sail plan, showing the cutter rig; two headsails and a mainsail.

Paddy Barry and Jarlath setting up the first frames.

In building *Northabout*, all components were selected as the best on offer for the task, bearing in mind the funds available. For that reason a well-engineered hull would be built. The mast, sails and rigging needed to be stronger than normal. So much would depend on the reliability of the engine and machinery, and we gave our utmost attention to their selection and installation.

Our policy was to keep everything as simple as possible, because the more complex the system the greater the difficulty in the event of a breakdown. We had a constant dilemma selecting the best materials available, within our limited funds. This required ongoing ingenuity and hard work in sourcing components.

To survive in the treacherous Arctic, one must eat well, and keep warm and dry. *Northabout* would be heated by a Dickenson diesel stove, which also would be used to cook and, to bake our daily bread. As a back-up, a two-burner propane stove would be also fitted and we would carry eight 25kg gas cylinders, propane doesn't freeze as readily as butane.

1,850 litres of Arctic grade diesel would be carried in five separate tanks, each entirely self-contained in case any tank was contaminated. The entire hull would be insulated to prevent heat loss.

On *Northabout* the headsails would have roller furling for ease of handling and the mainsail would have three sets of reef points. The mast would be equipped with steps enabling the more agile crew members to climb the mast for maintenance or to check ice leads ahead.

Safety in situations such as ours is of paramount importance; each crew member would be provided with a survival suit and life jacket. An eight-man life raft would be carried, along with a fibreglass dinghy and an inflatable dinghy. An Emergency Positioning Indicating Radio Beacon (EPIRB) would be carried, as would a High Frequency (HF) radio for long-distance radio transmission, a Very High Frequency (VHF) radio, a back-pack emergency HF radio and spare radios to duplicate all.

The machinery spares would include starter, alternator, all engine hoses and gaskets, two spare propellers, flexible couplings, propeller puller, oil, oil filters, diesel filters and much more including all sizes of nuts and bolts.

Our navigation equipment would include two fixed Global Positioning Systems (GPS) (a satellite-based navigation system made up of a network of 24 satellites placed into orbit by the US Department of Defense), two hand-held GPS, radar, compass and hand-bearing compasses, and paper charts for the entire route. Three years later, for the North East Passage, we would upgrade to a chart plotter linked to GPS, with paper charts, parallel rules and dividers as back-up. For emergency battery charging we carried a solar panel and a small, petrol-operated generator.

The boat was designed for construction in either steel or aluminium. We decided to build in aluminium. As I was working mainly single-handed, the lighter weight of alloy was a great attraction. I could fabricate all the frames and lift them without help. Another attraction of alloy is that it can be cut with the woodworking machinery I already had available. Also, as it doesn't rust, it would not show the scratches and dents from ice.

Building *Northabout*

The boat-building process began in February 2000, by setting out (lofting) all fifteen frames full size onto sheets of plywood.

Paddy and I did this setting-out at nights after work in the site offices of a construction project in Dublin. We made plywood patterns of each of the frames, which were used later as patterns for marking out the alloy frames. This saved a lot of time later when construction began in earnest.

I retired from my day job in April 2000. My knees were giving me trouble for many years; my orthopaedic surgeon had done some repairs to keep me mobile and now suggested a replacement knee as the only solution. I was reluctant to submit myself to this drastic and irreversible operation when I learned of the limited life of the replacement joints. With care, away from the hectic activity of large construction sites, I felt my original knees could last for many more years.

As I had never welded aluminium previously, I took a crash course in MIG welding. MIG (Metal Inert Gas) uses an aluminium alloy wire as a combined electrode and filler material. The filler metal is added continuously and welding without filler material is therefore not possible. Since the welding machine controls all welding parameters, the process is also called semi-automatic welding. I was pleased when my test welding passed all the laboratory tests, as the integrity of the welding would be severely tested in the Arctic later.

Construction of the boat began in my late father's unused joinery workshop in Mayo on Good Friday 2000. *Northabout* was the biggest object built there in its 50-year history, during which time many interesting projects had been completed. When the time came to move the boat out of the workshop it would be necessary to enlarge the door opening. This would be dealt with later, much to the amusement of the neighbours who thought we had overlooked this problem. One of the advantages of working in the construction industry is that one gets to know the right man for the job and a contact I knew with a giant concrete saw solved this challenge without difficulty.

I have always had a fascination with building boats. Boat building is an art, and to see a hull form emerge from a craftsman's hands is for me one of life's great miracles. The hull of *Northabout*

Top: *The hull was built upside down in a workshop. The hull was then hauled out by forklift truck to an awaiting crane.* Right: *Turning the hull over with the crane was a very delicate operation, requiring great care to ensure no damage occurred.*

was built upside down. First, I fabricated the fifteen frames that formed its shape; these were then positioned accurately on their pre-marked positions on the floor. The frames were then plumbed and temporarily braced in position. When stringers were added, the boat shape emerged like a vision, each day's progress clearly visible. As I was working on my own, lifting the full-length plates was a problem. This was solved by 'borrowing' some willing members of the local football team for a 'quick lift' on their way home from training. I also organised the work to enable the team to assist with particular events on some weekends.

I made full-sized plywood patterns of the hull panels and, from these patterns, marked out the aluminium panels. This ensured I made no costly errors when I cut the aluminium. As a result the hull was fair and without bumps.

When all the panels were tack-welded in place, the welding proper began. There followed weeks of careful welding using the MIG process, first inside, then outside, followed by grinding all protruding welds. In the meantime, Frank had organised the building of the rudder and centreboard case in Dublin. The centre plate was machined in an engineering shop in Galway, the stainless steel exhaust assembly fabricated by Terry's friends in Belfast, and the rudder bearings machined by Frank's friends in Dundalk. A truly all-Ireland team effort! Paddy, from his office in Dublin, continued to expedite the delivery of materials to Mayo.

Hull-turning day was a landmark event in the building

The hull, ready for decking and fitting out.

process. The hull was hauled outside and turned over by hired mobile crane. There was no resting on our laurels, or slackening in the activity; it was immediately hauled back into the workshop for engine fitting, decking, and interior fit out. The list of outstanding tasks to be dealt with seemed endless. Some of the major items to be tackled included fitting six tons of internal lead ballast, spraying insulation, fitting electrical and electronic equipment, steering gear, fitting hatches and windows, gas installation, plumbing, fuel tanks, upholstery and the most important item, the cooker. To assist with the interior fit-out a carpenter, Francois, was employed, while I continued the other work.

With the departure date edging ever closer, the pressure to complete the project grew even more intense and many long nights were spent in the workshop under floodlights.

Finally, after fifteen months work, *Northabout* was lifted onto a low-loader and transported 30 miles to Westport where she was launched on 9 June 2001. The road journey went smoothly, despite *Northabout*'s 'abnormal load' status. We were given a police escort through the narrow streets of Westport, where the Garda on duty stopped the traffic 'with one wave of his hand' and waved us through.

After launching, there was still much work to be done. Placing the mast nearly brought disaster on us. The hire charges on the crane being foremost in our minds, we were anxious to release the crane. Not enough care was taken in securing the temporary rigging to the deck fittings. When the crane released its slings from the mast, a temporary rigging fitting supporting the mast failed and down came the mast into the water! Fortunately the mast had a soft landing in the water without

Clockwise from top left: *John McClintock, the great grandson of Leopold McClintock, the explorer, performed the naming ceremony; Fr Brian Cronin prayed for God's blessing on* Northabout; *Ciara Cronin assists in the blessing; the blessing ceremony. Left to right: Michael Brogan, Fr Brian Cronin, Kevin Cronin, Paddy Barry; John McClintock about to break a bottle of champagne on* Northabout's *bow.*

Clockwise from top: Northabout *underway at last with Mayo flag flying at bow; sailing past Croagh Patrick; pursued by photographers. (Courtesy Shay Fennelly)*

Clockwise from top left: *a group of friends came to see us off; taking on two tons of food and drink for two seasons in the Arctic at Westport Quay; our friends take a short sail with us.*
(Courtesy Shay Fennelly)

damage or, worse still, without hitting anybody. The mast was recovered from the water and re-stepped immediately, and this time we took care to ensure it was more securely rigged before the crane was released.

The next two weeks were a frantic frenzy of activity. Fitting-out continued: engine controls were linked up, sails fitted, and on the Thursday evening before our planned Saturday departure, we had our first sail around Clew Bay. This was a momentous occasion; the sailing conditions were perfect and *Northabout* sailed beautifully. But there was still much to be done, not least to mention loading 1,800 litres of diesel, food and drink for two seasons, safety equipment, spares for everything and spares for the spares.

On the evening of Saturday 23 June 2001 *Northabout* took on the last of its supplies: duty-free stores of 1,000 cans of beer and 72 bottles of whiskey. Well, it would be a long time before a pub would be seen again!

We were honoured to have John McClintock, great-grandson of the great polar explorer Leopold McClintock, perform the naming ceremony with the traditional bottle of champagne, followed by Fr Brian Cronin's prayer – he sought God's blessing on the boat, its crew, its engine, its anchor and its cooker. Fr Brian was assisted by Ciara Cronin who, with a sprig of an ash tree – sacred to the Celts – dispensed water from Saint Brigid's well, and read a special blessing from the

The journey begins. After a hectic building programme of fifteen months, Northabout *is on its way, on the first stage of the voyage to Greenland. (Courtesy Shay Fennelly)*

native Inuits of the Alaskan territories for a safe journey. Thus fortified, at 19.30 hours and, in perfect conditions *Northabout* left Westport Quay, with a large gathering of friends and well-wishers waving their goodbyes.

This was the start of its voyage to the Pacific. *Northabout* sailed west out the winding channel into the sunset, escorted by a flotilla of boats from Mayo Sailing Club, with bonfires blazing, and music playing – what better start could there be?

As we sailed in a gentle breeze towards Clare Island at the entrance to Clew Bay, Michael Brogan cooked us all a farewell steak dinner. The past few weeks had taken their toll on me. I was completely worn out trying to get everything on the boat working properly. I needed a rest! Within sight of Granuaile's castle on Clare Island, Michael and I shook hands with Paddy and the crew. Michael and I then transferred to our friend's yacht, Seamus Salmon's *Saoirse*, and bade *Northabout* farewell. We would join them in Greenland in a month's time.

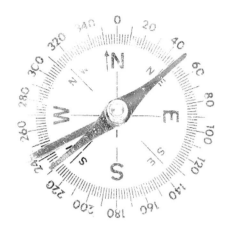

3

BRIEF HISTORY
OF THE SEARCH FOR THE
NORTH WEST PASSAGE

The search for the North West Passage began in earnest in the early nineteenth century, as the British Admiralty sought a northern route from the North Atlantic to the Pacific. The allure of the treasures of Cathay (China) and the prospect of Russia or another nation finding the route, initiated a frenzy of exploration to find the elusive route. A northern route would avoid the long and dangerous southern route around Cape Horn or Africa's Cape of Good Hope.

With plenty of manpower and ships available, and no major enemies to quell, several British expeditions were despatched to find a North West Passage.

The North West Passage extends from Greenland's Melville Bay to Baffin Bay on Canada's east coast, thence via Lancaster Sound, Peel Sound, Simpson Strait and through the route north of Canada and Alaska to Point Barrow in the Bering Straits.

Little by little, the early explorers gradually mapped the area, by sea and by land, adding to the

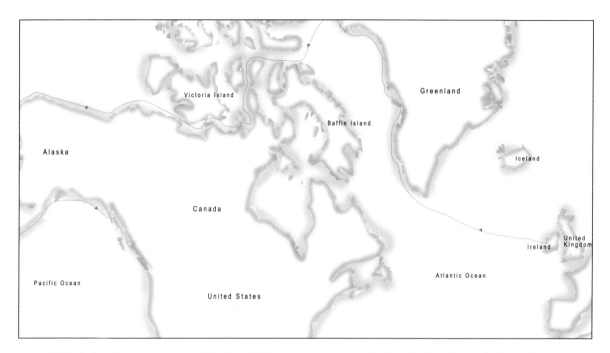

Map of Northabout's *voyage in 2001. The North West Passage starts at Baffin Island and extends through the twisting channels north of Canada and Alaska, ending at Barrow, the most northerly point of Alaska.*

knowledge gained, at the cost of great loss of life and human suffering.

The obvious problem in Arctic exploration is, of course, the freezing sea and harsh weather, with winter temperatures of minus 50 degrees frequently recorded.

The sea is frozen for most of the year, breaking up for a few short weeks in August and early September. Even when the ice does break up, the floes drift with the wind. A gale can cause ice floes to drift down on unwieldy ships, trapping, squeezing and crushing everything in their path. Apart from drifting ice and pressure ice, the explorers' ships were frequently beset in new ice. Falling temperatures caused the sea to freeze around them. Overwintering in the beset ships was a common occurrence, the unfortunate sailors having to exist on inadequate ships' rations. The attraction of double pay may explain why sailors risked their lives on these polar voyages.

Almost invariably scurvy decimated the ship's crew. Inexplicably, the causes of scurvy were misunderstood by the Admiralty, even up to the time of Shackleton's and Scott's expeditions. Yet Captain Cook, 100 years earlier, knew that fresh fruit and vegetables contained the unknown missing ingredient. It is now known that lack of vitamin C is the cause of scurvy. In 1747 the Scottish naval surgeon James Lind treated scurvy-ridden sailors with lemons and oranges and obtained dramatic cures. By 1795 the British Navy began to distribute regular rations of lime juice to sailors on long sea voyages, hence British sailors were called Limeys. Unfortunately, on the Arctic voyages, the lime juice they used was concentrated, which destroyed the vitamin C. Scurvy does not occur in most animals, as they can synthesise their own vitamin C. The Inuit get their vitamin C mainly

from eating raw meat, especially from the organs of seals.

By 1846 expeditions from both the Atlantic and Pacific sides of North America had mapped most of the route by sea and by overland explorations, leaving only about 500 miles in the middle unexplored. To complete the work, the Admiralty dispatched their biggest ever and best-equipped expedition under the command of Sir John Franklin with two ships, the *Erebus* and *Terror*. Franklin was familiar with some of the shores of northern Canada, having previously taken part in three overland expeditions to map the area.

The *Erebus* and *Terror* never returned, nor were the crew ever seen alive again. This is one of the great unsolved exploration mysteries. It is generally believed their tinned food was of such poor quality that it may have caused malnutrition or botulism. Another theory suggests the soldered tins may have caused lead poisoning.

Top: *Sir John Franklin, the leader of the lost expedition which set out in 1845 to find the North West Passage. (Courtesy National Maritime Museum)* Above: *Engraving of Franklin's ships the* Erebus *and* Terror *in a storm.*

25

Gjoa, *Roald Amundsen's converted herring fishing boat, was the first vessel to sail through the North West Passage. This is a copy of a painting for* Gjoa *which hangs in the Tromso polar museum.*

It is true that the tinned meat was delivered late, leaving no time to check the quality, and some tins left behind in England were putrid when examined.

The searches that followed eventually pieced together some of the Franklin mystery and in the process the route through the North West Passage was discovered but not sailed. Captain McClure sledged through the final unknown miles in 1853.

Eventually the Norwegian explorer Roald Amundsen became the first person to sail through the North West Passage in his vessel, the converted herring boat *Gjoa*.

The passage took three years, from 1903 to 1906. *Gjoa* spent two winters in the sheltered bay where the settlement of Gjoahaven is now located, and a third winter at King Point near Herschel Island. Amundsen lived with the native Inuit people and learned much from them on how to survive in the frozen wastes, which later helped him on his South Pole expedition. Knud Rasmussen completed the passage by dog sledge from Greenland to the Bering Strait in 1923-24.

Northabout *sailing through ice; this photograph shows some of the hazards of sailing in polar regions.*

Remarkably, no other vessel got through until Canada's Captain Larsen on the 80-ton schooner *St Roch* made the transit in 1940 to 1942 from the Pacific to the Atlantic. After refitting and installing a more powerful engine he made the return passage in one season in 1944.

Since then, several transits were made by Canadian and US warships and icebreakers.

But it wasn't until 1977 that the next small vessel attempted the passage. The transit was a remarkable one undertaken by the yacht *Williwaw* in 1977 under the command of the Belgian adventurer Willi De Roos. He sailed through in one season, mainly single-handed, a remarkable voyage by a remarkably tough man.

In 2001, *Northabout* was the thirteenth small vessel to complete the passage.

Captain Larsen, travelling in the St Roch, transited the North West Passage in 1940 and again in 1942. The St Roch is preserved in the maritime museum in Vancouver, Canada.

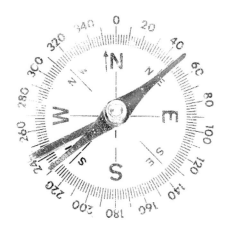

4

WESTPORT TO GREENLAND

PADDY BARRY

Passage to Greenland

With dusk changed to darkness we lay off in the channel between Clare Island and Dooega Head on Achill. The half-tide rock, Deaces, was given a respectful berth. The breeze was light as we ghosted along at three and a half knots or so. Over on Achill, by the village of Keel, bonfires blazed, for it was the eve of St John's Day. This celebration is not confined to Ireland. In 1990, sailing 300 miles north of Iceland, we had joined a group of Norwegians around a bonfire on St John's Eve on the island of Jan Mayen. Much of what we fondly imagine is peculiarly Irish is in fact universal throughout the north Atlantic. A thousand years ago, the monks of Ireland and the warriors of Scandinavia, sometimes with their captives from Ireland, sailed through these waters. Their joint imprint is still clear in the folklore, the writings, the remains and more recently the analysis of DNA records. These are our waters, our front door to the world, to the Americas and beyond. Our back door opens merely to the continent of Europe; important, yes, but lacking the grandeur of the waters and the lands we were facing.

Shortly after midnight we emerged into the open ocean, Achill Island behind us and the Black

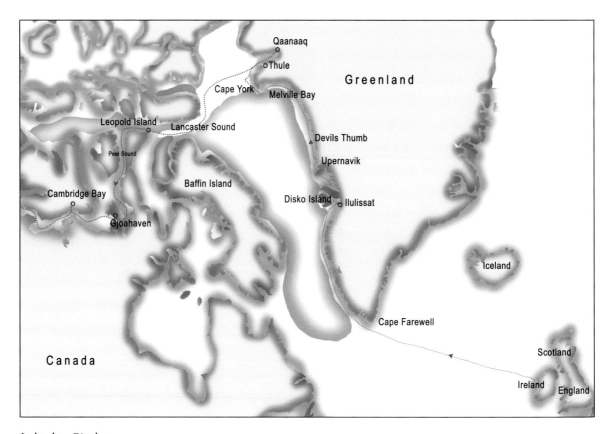

Ireland to Gjoahaven.

Rock lighthouse to its north flashing every twelve seconds. That all faded further to our stern as the wind freshened from the south west, cool but a good sailing wind for us.

We set into our sea-going watches. Although nobody sleeps much for the first couple of nights it is important to establish a routine, who is on and who is off, and when, and who gets called if there is an incident, and indeed what constitutes an incident. In all of this, and in going through the safety routines, there lies a balance between tedious reviewing of every possible contingency and its (ideal) consequent action and a more *laissez faire*, or even cavalier view that we all know what we're at.

My first long passage was in 1986, sailing the trade wind route in *Saint Patrick* from Tenerife to Bermuda. We were going to a tall ships gathering in New York to celebrate the bicentennial of the Statue of Liberty. That had been our first real ocean passage – 3,000 miles. On that passage we did everything by the book, every last eventuality was anticipated and prepared for. Practically the order in which we would board our life raft was predetermined and certainly the essential stores and equipment that was to be brought if needs be. I remember Kevin being warned that he wouldn't be allowed into the life raft without the five-gallon drum of fresh water, which was his charge.

Left: *Paddy Barry, the skipper of the famed Galway Hooker,* St Patrick, *and the leader of the* Northabout *North West Passage expedition.*
Below: *Galway Hookers racing;* St Patrick *and* MacDuach *battle for supremacy.*

31

This time round, we weren't quite so detailed in that part of our preparations. That night we merely set the watches. Tomorrow we would go through the safety drill.

The watches were set with two crew on watch, Gearóid Ó Riain with Pat Redmond, Paddy Barry with Harry Connolly, Cathal De Barra with Eoin Coyle.

Let's meet them:

Gearóid, now approaching the age of 30, had been a student when we first sailed together thirteen or fourteen years earlier. From the earliest times afloat with me he had shown aptitude in mechanics and electrics. In the meantime he had become a hot shot on computers, emails, sending photos through the air and all that sort of thing. He called it Information Technology, IT. Magic, I called it.

Pat Redmond was a sailor and climber. Orienteer, whistle-player, cricketer, Gaelic footballer earlier, little had escaped his attention. His sailing had been at championship level in the GP 14 class sailing dinghy. I had introduced him to cruising, sailing around Ireland, Scotland and the Baltic, to which he applied himself with enthusiasm and enjoyment.

Eoin Coyle came on board to fill the vacancy caused by the absence of his father John, who had to drop out due to time pressure. This may not be seen as much of a way to engage crew. But it worked for Eoin and it worked for us. It happened that John Coyle couldn't travel. We lost John, but gained Eoin, fresh at eighteen years of age from sitting his Leaving Certificate exams. His real education was only beginning.

Harry Connolly is from Dublin but has lived and worked in Luxemburg for many years, on EU media. As a state employee he has long holidays and has always used them to full effect, whether climbing in the Alps or sailing. He had been with me in Greenland in 1993, sailing and climbing. Then, sailing in ice-strewn waters, he always took to his sleeping bag fully dressed for evacuation. No way was Harry going to be caught out on the ice in his y-fronts!

The fourth member of the 'delivery crew', as they called themselves, was my son Cathal De Barra. Experienced canoeist and outdoorsman, lawyer by day, he had previously taken a year out to backpack, before it was common to do so. This was his first ocean passage.

All Saturday night we sailed gently away westwards. By daylight on Sunday morning the land had gone; now it was ocean all round. A southerly wind freshened; we close reached and flew in fine style, although we all felt queasy. By next day we had our 'sea-legs', laughing and cooking, and continued sailing until Monday evening when the wind fell off. We found the boat to sail well. She got speed up to 6 knots easily, and with stronger wind and sail set correctly, got to 8 knots.

Teething problems were few; so far, the starboard topmast spreader needed its end cap re-fixed to keep the shroud from jumping out. That needed a man up the mast but in a fairly flat sea it was easily enough done.

The weather forecast, coming in over the radio fax, was for 24 hours of calm, then a south-easterly from a slow-moving low pressure system to the south of our track. In the meantime we continued northwest under engine, rigged the reefing pennants, fixed fire extinguishers in place, built shelves and generally continued sorting things out. The inside of the boat became increasingly 'liveable' with less of the 'thrown together' feeling.

The boat technology was working a treat, with the autopilot doing most of the steering and the Single Side Band Radio (SSB) making reliable contact. One of the gas rings wasn't working, but you'd have to leave something for fixing later!

On Wednesday the wind blew, cool and off the quarter, in grey seas. That low pressure had deepened and we sailed hard and fast. There was a balance between testing the boat and rig for any weakness, and then again, not overdoing it. Increasingly our confidence in the rig grew. We tightened the lee shrouds as the sea swept the deck at our feet, well harnessed for this.

It continued so and on Thursday we lit the Dickenson stove. What a difference it made inside the boat, so warm and cosy – deceptively so – as only feet away, the seas swept the deck, grey and cold. No matter; we were doing about 7 knots continuously, about 170 miles a day. Greenland was now only a few hundred miles away.

On Friday morning, still with wind astern, we had two reefs in the mainsail and had the headsail poled out. The glass had dropped as we passed closer to that low-pressure centre but what a different world it is when it's from astern and not from ahead. Pat baked our first bread in the Dickenson stove that day – Odlums brown bread mix – voted by all as a culinary success, which was just as well as we had an enormous amount on board.

The humour all round was good and why wouldn't it be? With such progress behind us it was then only 380 miles to Cape Farewell and all systems were working well. We ran the engine twice a day for half an hour to keep the batteries charged, and plotted our course both by Satellite GPS and in the old-fashioned, manual way.

Later that day the wind fell light and watch distances fell to only 14 miles, as compared to our previous good ones of 30 miles. At midnight someone wrote in the log:

'This evening, after dinner, we had a magnificent sunset, the boat sailed down a silver road set out by the evening sun's rays.'

Saturday was uneventful until the third watch, some time after 08.00. The wind came up, out of the north, the seas got greyer and the Dickenson blew out. We reefed down and rolled the head-sail and sailed onto our first Greenland chart. The forecast came in from Narsarssuaq Greenland weather centre, a force eight from the north. And sure enough that was what blew, 35 knots. We pulled down a second reef, rolled the big genoa sail and unfurled the stronger inner foresail, and sailed right on through it. Happily for us the wind was on our beam.

With that snug rig we sailed through the night. The odd white wave-top crashed into the side of the boat with a great bang. Mostly the waves slid harmlessly beneath us.

On Sunday at 15.00 we sighted Cape Farewell ahead. An hour later, as visibility improved, the mountains opened to view, 30 miles off, magnificent and harsh, black rock and white ice and snow. We shook out the reefs and steered towards the shore, preparing potatoes and steak for dinner.

There was light broken sea ice, about 1/10, around us. Was it like this all the way to shore?

Qaqortoq Radio said no, it wasn't, and we knew that anyway. In early summer a dense band of glacier ice is carried southward on the east Greenland current and is swept some several hundred miles round Cape Farewell up the west coast.

The town of Nanortalik lay invitingly inshore of this ice. We considered going for it, and indeed tried. The ice thickened to 5/10 or 6/10. But this 'storis' ice was sharp and heaved threateningly in the swell. All notions of a 'nipped' vessel rising in this stuff are nonsense. 'Mangled' would be the effect of being caught in this. We withdrew.

All next day we motored north into the Davis Strait, outside the edge of the storis ice. The wind blew from the north, a gentle enough force 3 or 4. We could have taken a long tack seaward but we still had notions of getting inshore through the ice at first chance. The town of Qaqortoq now was abeam.

On Tuesday at 01.00, we were still motoring north outside the ice, when the engine stopped. We bled the fuel system of air and restarted. By dawn the ice had cleared inshore and we altered course for Arsuk fiord. Then the wind rose, this time against us. The forecast was for a force 9, from the northeast, and sure enough, we got it. The sea rose, and the wind blew the tops off it. We were now only 10 miles or so off the land, with the wind blowing off.

But could we make progress towards it? We couldn't. Neither with sail nor with the engine at high revs could we get ahead. We kept getting blown off. The boat, which had behaved so well until now, just couldn't handle the strong headwind. Her high freeboard and shallow hull made for too much top hamper (boat above the water) in these conditions.

We bore away to the west-northwest, engine off and pulling under small headsail. This was a different world; it always is with the wind astern. The odd iceberg was in sight, spaced as they were at three or four miles apart, no problem for us and for the new hands wonderful to behold, indeed for all of us. At our speed of six to nine knots they came up frequently.

We came all too close to hitting one of them though. Running downwind. It lay directly ahead of us, increasingly closer. However, whichever way I turned the wheel, the sail altered or the engine revved, we just couldn't get our head away from it. The grace of God and some kind of backwind off the berg carried us clear, with about two metres to spare. After that we hove to, lashing the steering down and carrying only a handkerchief of sail we lay quietly on the port tack. Now she lay pointing just slightly upwind, drifting at 2 or 2½ knots to the northwest. We tracked the bergs on radar and no further avoiding action was necessary.

On Wednesday 4 July a Royal Greenland Ship passed bound for Denmark. As the wind fell, we sighted a humpback whale and we made through the narrow rocky entrance into the town of Paamuit. We tied alongside the jetty, got into our bunks and slept.

Later, we rose easily and breakfasted through the day. We were too late for the town bakery but a mini-market was open. Cathal was despatched to the Police Station with our passports to make our presence known.

He enquired from the Police Chief, a buxom lady, where he might get a beer?

'How about my place,' she suggested. Greenland can be like that.

We had some fix-ups to do on the boat but, all in all, very few. The steering cables had become somewhat slack and needed tightening, though not much more. The boat had come through with flying colours; a ten-day passage in varying conditions was not at all bad – better than planned for – and now we had plenty of time to make the 600 odd miles up the coast to Illulisat by 20 July, where we would have our crew change.

Those Greenland Days

Ice axes, crampons, rucksacks and ropes came out. We were now on our holidays!

Each day we sailed gently northwards, the days grew longer and the weather got better. We anchored in fjords and climbed the high hills. In the wonderful clear air distances are deceptive. What looks 10km is probably 20, a hill that looks 700 metres is probably double that. No matter; the days were long and mostly sunny. Greenland is well mapped by the Danish. The 1:250,000 maps are fine for trekking or climbing.

The major climbing areas are to the south around the Tasermuit and Prins Kristian fjord area – good

Northabout *at anchor.*

rock, steep spires and pinnacles, mostly still unclimbed. All along the west coast there are fjords to lose oneself in, valleys to trek and hills to climb.

Lief Erickson, Eric the Red, wasn't being deceptive 1,000 years ago when he named this place Greenland; the valleys really are green; for a few weeks in summer at any rate. And amid this greenery flowers abound.

The Greenlanders have a song, *Nasimi*, which translated goes

Give me a flower, give me a flower
O my loved one
Give me a flower before the summer's gone
Give me a flower, give me a flower
O my loved one
For in Greenland the summers are so short.

Greenlanders love music and love to sing, and unfortunately for many of them, love to drink too much.

There are 55,000 people in Kalaat Nunaat, 'land of the people', all living on the coast. The inland ice cap is bare and devoid of game and seal on which they lived until recent times. Most of the population live on the south-west coast, with towns every 100 miles or so. There are some villages, or settlements, in between but not many. The Danish government for several hundred years have ruled Greenland benignly as a colony. Since the 1960s, in attempting to improve schooling, medical care and such, the Danes encouraged the population to move into the towns. Though well intentioned, this has not sat well with the Greenlandic way of life, that of hunters and independent people. Nowhere is this incongruity more apparent than in the capital Nuuk, where 10 per cent of Greenland's population live. Many live in Copenhagen-style apartment blocks and it doesn't suit them at all.

Our journey was not a sociology study though – we take things as we find them, talk to who will talk to us, enjoy the country and the seas around and have a few beers in the café if there is one.

And so, over the following fortnight, we sailed and climbed calling in to Fiskenes, Nuuk and Manitsoq. We fished and caught Arctic char and saw minke whale being hunted by the locals. At

Sisimuit, north of the Arctic Circle, we met our first huskies, working sled dogs. These dogs are serious carnivores, kept chained, and should be photographed with telephoto lenses. You are much more likely to be eaten by a husky than by a bear.

Qeqertasuaq Island in Danish is called Disko and in Greenlandic, suaq means big, siaq means small. With Home Rule most of the Danish names have, in the last ten years reverted to their original. The Danes have retained Foreign Policy and Defence but have handed over autonomy in most other matters to the Greenlanders.

And who are the Greenlanders? Ten per cent are pure Inuit, or Eskimo, as they used to be called. These are hunters to this day, speaking only Greenlandic, keeping very much to themselves, still shooting and butchering the seal to feed their families. They do not use kayaks any more and why should they, when the ubiquitous open fibreglass 18-footer and 40 horsepower outboard motors are available.

Seal meat tastes strong and is best eaten, we found, with plenty of onion and curry.

Eighty per cent of the population are mixed race – Inuit with varying lesser component of Danish and white blood: the whalers who never went home. Knud Rasmussen is the most esteemed of these, Danish father and Inuit mother. And 10 per cent are Danes, not really Greenlanders. They are the doctors and engineers, the contract construction workers, the senior administrators. They are mostly on short-duration contracts and, we found, tend to have a love-hate relationship with the country.

Some nurses we spoke to said that, if you have an accident and can speak only one sentence, say 'Take me to the airport'!

Yet Gretel Erlich, the previous doctor in Illulisat hospital, had written a wonderfully descriptive book, *This Cold Heaven,* in Danish. It was later translated into English.

In Qeqertassuaq Island, in 1857, Leopold McClintock had stopped in the vessel *Fox* when setting out on yet another of the searches for the lost Franklin expedition. McClintock wrote of this area: 'I do not know of a more enticing spot for a week's fishing, shooting and yachting.'

He obviously didn't go trekking. We did a multi-day hike, and the mosquitoes nearly ate us alive whenever there was no wind. Apart from that it was magnificent: big valleys, stone and grass, shining streams,

Greenland working dog.

Northabout *in brash ice.*

some to be crossed waist deep! The maps show the old winter sledging routes; these invariably make the best trekking routes too, with the added interest of coming across the odd discard from a hunter's sledge. We camped where they had, lighting our cooking fire with grass and driftwood, and sleeping under the open sky. Meanwhile, Gearóid had dived beneath the boat, through ice, to fix the boat's centreboard lifting strop.

All too soon this idyll in Arctic arcadia was over. Illulisat and the incoming crew called.

In easy wind we sailed the 70 miles across Disko Bay. We passed the big Illulisat glacier, its front a mile long, calving icebergs with thunderous roar. We sailed in through the dense brash ice from the bergs (another little test for the boat, 100 per cent for the welds) and on Sunday 21 July, Pat, Harry, Eoin and Cathal left for Copenhagen and home.

5

GREENLAND

Kevin Cronin, Michael Brogan, John Murray, Frank Nugent, Terry Irvine and I flew to Illulisat on the west coast of Greenland, to catch up with *Northabout*. Paddy and the crew had sailed from Ireland on her 'sea trials' as we light-heartedly described the 2,000-mile Atlantic crossing. At Kangerlussuaq airport, where we changed planes, we crossed paths with the home-going crew, Pat Redmond, Eoin Coyle, Cathal De Barra and Harry Connolly, all looking the worse for wear from partying the previous couple of nights. After they left on a flight to Copenhagen, a short flight brought us to Illulisat where *Northabout* was secure and snug in the tiny harbour. All was well aboard – Paddy Barry and Gearóid O'Riain welcomed us. I was pleased to see many small improvements were completed, the storage improved, and many small items incomplete on leaving Westport were now finished. The centreboard lifting mechanism, which had been giving trouble, was improved and re-rigged.

Illulisat (Jakobshavn) is sheltered from the west wind by Disko Island. It has the most prolific glacier in Greenland, constantly calving icebergs into the bay, which then drift across Baffin Bay, south to Labrador and on to warmer waters, where they gradually melt and finally expire. The

A seal hunter: kayaks are still used for seal hunting in Greenland and they are individually made to suit the size of the paddler.

incessant thunderous noise of the bergs breaking off the glacier can be disquieting. A huge wave is generated as the bergs fall into the sea, with further waves forming when chunks break off the bergs. The rule when sailing in Arctic waters is simple; keep well away from icebergs as they are constantly changing their centre of gravity; a seemingly stable iceberg can roll over without warning.

The weather was a bright and a sunny 16 degrees, warmer than home, and unlike my vision of Greenland. Swarms of mosquitoes attacked the newcomers with a vengeance. How do mosquitoes survive the cold winters here? Survive they do and thrive; in Alaska the mosquito is called the national bird. Soon my face and arms were covered in bites, which developed into huge lumps. At the first opportunity I bought a very effective hat with combined mosquito net, which solved the mosquito problem.

Illulisat has a strong link with the Franklin expedition; the last communications the outside world received from John Franklin, the commander of *Erebus* and *Terror*, were dispatched in July 1845 from this very place. From here Franklin and the crew wrote their last letters home. These letters were taken back to England by the stores transport ship, *Baretto Junior*, which accompanied the expedition to Greenland.

Before leaving Illulisat we visited the house in which the explorer and anthropologist Knud Rasmussen was born in 1879. This remarkable man was known throughout Greenland as Kununnguaq

(Little Knud). Knud was the son of the local pastor and an Inuit woman. He learned the Inuit language from his mother, learning Danish later at school. From an early age he could handle a dog sled and rifle and learned to survive like the local hunters. He attended college at the university of Copenhagen in Denmark. In 1902 he joined the Ludvig Mylius-Erichsen literary expedition to northern Greenland, where his talent as a writer was discovered. His knowledge in translating the Inuit language was indispensable to the expedition – he could hold conversations with the local tribes and re-tell them in Danish. He wrote his first book, *The New People*, about the Eskimos in the Melville Bay region, the first of his many books.

Later, with Peter Freuchen, he led most of the 'Thule Expeditions'. He will be remembered as the first man to dog sled the North West Passage from Greenland to the Bering Strait. His kindness and understanding of the Inuit people and his fight for their rights have made him a national hero. Knud fostered a deep understanding between Greenland and Denmark – without him many of the Inuit stories and legends would have been lost forever. He died in 1933 of food poisoning.

After taking on stores, *Northabout* sailed out amidst the brash ice through the channel north of Disko Island, the Vaigat, known as iceberg alley. Dodging the larger bergy bits, we sailed through the brash ice into the fog, making our way north to Upernavik, the largest Greenlandic settlement at this high latitude.

Upernavik, with a population of 3,000, was a hive of activity. Work was progressing in constructing a new harbour and the hill overlooking the harbour was bulldozed level to construct a new airport runway. *Northabout* moored alongside the dock near the new fish-processing plant.

The newly-painted and colourful houses perched in terraces, seemingly at random on the rocky hills, were a delightful contrast to the drab apartment blocks we had seen in the capital city of Nuuk.

Ashore, in the town square outside the hospital, uninvited, our musicians gave an impromptu concert, watched by curious children and a small group of bewildered adults under the watchful eye of two vigilant policemen.

The crew of Bob Shipton's well-travelled Scottish yacht, *Dodo's Delight,* joined us in the merry-making and dancing. Bob was on a climbing and sailing voyage to Bylot Island, with a group of experienced climbers. They planned to traverse the island north to south. Sadly, since then, Bob lost *Dodo's Delight* to an on-board fire in 2005 while overwintering in the ice near Upernavik.

Brendan Minish, our radio base man back home in Ireland sent us updates on ice charts via our HF radio linked to laptop computer. Melville Bay was reasonably clear of ice. Lancaster Sound, which is normally ice free by mid-July, was still locked solid with $9/10$ ice cover, so with Lancaster Sound impassable, we decided to take advantage of the time on our hands and use the opportunity to detour to the Thule area north of Baffin Bay, while we waited for conditions to improve.

As we made our way north we were hailed by a small boat. On board was the hunter Peter Aronson, an old friend of Paddy's, who had befriended him here in 1993. Peter spent two weeks as guide on Paddy's boat, *St Patrick,* as they tried unsuccessfully to cross Melville Bay. He invited

Bob Shipton's yacht, Dodo's Delight, *secured outside* Northabout *in Upernavik Harbour, Greenland.*

us to Tussaaq, his nearby island home. Peter is now the only permanent resident; he refused all inducements to re-settle.

The kettle was soon boiling on the Primus stove. The 40 or so houses on the island are now abandoned – it is sad to witness the death of a community. Life for younger people on such a remote outpost cannot compete with the attractions of the bright lights of Upernavik. After tea, with much sign language, Peter gave us a gift of plastic flowers that still adorn *Northabout's* saloon. He was delighted with our gift of tea and coffee and, after a photography session, we were on our way again.

We sailed northwards to Kap Shackleton (named after Lord Edward Shackleton, not Ernest) on Agparssuit with its bird cliffs, eventually arriving in Kraulshaven where we tied up alongside the small jetty at 04.30.

The children of the primary school, attracted by the rare sight of a sailing yacht, were waiting on the dock, all 85 of them, or so it appeared to us. Michael entertained them with lively jigs on his fiddle. Sven, the teacher, a Dane who had taught there for the past 26 years, on hearing the music, suggested we give a 'proper' concert in the school. Michael led the way playing the fiddle,

Top: Inuit hunter we met at sea, where he was shooting seals.
Left: Tea in Peter Aronson's house on Tussaaq Island. Peter is the only permanent resident left on the island.

the children following the 'pied piper' into the school. Regrettably none of us had a camera to record the scene – a camera may have been intrusive though.

A lively concert developed, with an appreciative audience: Paddy and Frank singing songs, Michael on fiddle. Later, an elderly man borrowed Michael's fiddle and played some familiar Scottish music. Some of the older people got out on the floor, lined up and danced a Caledonian set. They told us it was their traditional dance; somewhere in the misty past, visiting Scottish whalers had passed on their dance to the native Greenlanders. In fact, the whalers were far more familiar with the Arctic than the British Admiralty.

When William Scorsby, a whaler and an exceptional Arctic navigator, offered the Admiralty his help and advice, he was snubbed. The attitude prevailing was: how could these rough ignorant men possibly help the world's greatest navy? Yet had these whalers been employed to explore these waters, the North West Passage could have been found much earlier.

The British Captain, John Ross, first encountered the Inuit near here in 1818. He called them 'the Arctic Highlanders'. The Inuit were so isolated at that time, they believed they were the only people on earth. They were amazed and fearful at the first sight of the naval ship. Gradually, as they overcame their fear, they had many questions. Had the visitors come from the moon they asked? On seeing the sails move, they imagined the ships were live creatures. Hadn't they wings? Why were seamen man-hauling sledges? Did they not have any dogs?

Leaving Kraulshaven, the next notable sight was Kuvdlordssuak and the 'Devil's Thumb' (Djaevelens Tommelfinger), a volcanic pillar visible for miles. Formed by erosion of the softer surrounding mountain, all that remains now is the harder core. Such peaks attract climbers. Paddy and Frank resolved to scale it. Next day they did. Some of the glory dissipated later when a local fourteen-year old boy was introduced to us and he had recently conquered the peak too!

Having read all the horror stories of Melville Bay – of crushed boats and stranded crew – we did-

Children playing at midnight in Kraulshaven.

Above: *Approaching the Devil's Thumb.*
Left: *Rory and Michael admiring the meteorite in the Natural History Museum in New York. The explorer, Peary, stole this meteorite and others from the Inuit who regarded it as a sacred object.*

n't expect easy going. True, the ice charts showed it to be relatively clear of ice. Progress was good, just dodging the occasional berg, sometimes sailing in fog; we worked our way past Sabine Island, and onwards to Cape York. A granite monument there commemorates Peary, the polar explorer.

Meteorite Island lay shrouded in fog; from here Peary 'lifted' the sacred meteorite that contained the Inuit's only source of iron. The meteorite was loaded onto Peary's ship and sold later for $40,000; a fortune at the time. In exchange, he gave the Inuit some metal knives and hatchets. The meteorite is now housed in the American Museum of Natural History in New York.

Terry was the first to see a polar bear, asleep on a berg – a magnificent animal. The bear took to the water and swam out to have a look at us, approaching inquisitively with nose sniffing. He seemed so natural in his own wild environment, so unlike polar bears in captivity.

At this time of year polar bears are dangerous. They are generally hungry because seals, their main source of food, are not available when the ice has broken up. They swim from floe to floe looking for seals and will attack a human when hungry. We carried a pair of shotguns, hoping the noise would scare them away. A Canadian hunter later advised me to saw off the barrels: 'that way it will be easier to shoot yourself if attacked, them peashooters will only antagonise bears.' Luckily that bear showed no more interest in us.

The earlier repair to the centreboard lifting mechanism had again failed; the board was now permanently in the down position. This did not matter here in Greenland's deep water but in the shallow passages of the Canadian coast it would be crucial to have the ability to raise the centre-board. To carry out permanent repairs we needed to get to a sheltered harbour, in calm water, and what better place than the American air base at Thule? In a good harbour we could expect every assistance from their well-equipped machine shops. How wrong can you be?

Sailing north into Melville Bay in northern Greenland.

Danish writer, explorer and anthropologist Knud Rasmussen founded the trading post of Thule in 1909. The area is also called North Star Bay, named after the ship *North Star* delivering Knud, who sought shelter there during a violent storm. They had not planned to make this their base but as it turned out it was the best suited in the district. Knud's life-long friend Peter Freuchen managed the trading post. Peter married Navarana, a native Inuit, and raised a family there, giving us a fine insight into Inuit life. His best-known book is *Ice Floes and Flaming Water; a True Adventure in Melville Bay.*

The trading post was unique in that all profits were used to fund scientific expeditions and Eskimo studies.

During the Cold War the Danish government leased the area to the US to build an air base, which is now part of the US network of early warning radars 750 miles north of the Arctic Circle, and home to the 821st Air Base Group. More controversially it is also the home of the 12th Space Warning Squadron, a unit of the Ballistic Missile Early Warning System designed to detect and track intercontinental ballistic missiles, and home also to part of the 50th Space Wing's global satellite control network.

Thule now has a 10,000-foot runway and the northernmost deepwater port in the world.

As we drew near Thule a patrol boat and two high-speed RIBs, manned by fully armed personnel in survival suits, approached us. They made it clear we were not welcome. After explaining our difficulty, we eventually got permission to tie alongside the huge dock. Under no circumstances could we go ashore and no assistance could be given. Our weapons were taken from us (two shotguns to scare bears), cartridges counted and confiscated, and receipts given. We were allowed 24 hours to carry out repairs.

Armed guards were posted; this amused us – that we should be considered a threat to such a powerful garrison.

Hiding our amusement, we got the repair complete in a couple of hours. The wire lifting strop had parted Gearóid 'volunteered to reattach a new stainless steel wire to the centreboard underwater, which he did in record time, helped no doubt by a desire to get out of the freezing water. Despite his wetsuit and scuba equipment, he was blue with the cold, though he recovered quickly after a hot meal and was ready for the music session that followed. On the dock above us, frozen soldiers patrolled with weapons at the ready.

In the morning we retrieved our ancient weapons and cartridges, signed off the receipt, and said 'goodbye, and thanks for all your help'. The reply was curt: 'You guys have a good trip, and don't come back.' We won't.

150 miles of hard sailing north brought us to Qaanaaq, an Inuit settlement in Inglefield Fjord. These people, who once happily lived in Thule, were moved north to 'new Thule' after the American 'invasion'. I cannot imagine a more unsuitable location for a settlement. Qaanaaq has no harbour, no shelter, nor good fishing or hunting.

The Inuit suffered the same heavy-handed mistreatment as the native people of the Aleutian Islands were subjected to during the Second World War, as we were to hear later.

A local Inuit man told me of their opposition to the American occupation of the Thule area, which they know as Pitugfiup or Pituffik. After Hitler's army overran Denmark in 1940, the Danish government handed over the security of Greenland to the US.

At Thule a harbour and an airfield were constructed, which played an important part in the war effort. Over 5,000 troops were stationed in Thule. After the war the base was redundant for a while. Because of the perceived Cold War threat in 1952 the base was reoccupied and further expanded. The Inuit population were forcibly relocated to Qaanaaq. The base officially had a defence role; in fact, offensive B-52 bombers were stationed there. This came to light when a B-52 crashed near Thule in January 1968 with four hydrogen bombs on board. The fragments of three bombs were recovered; the fourth bomb was lost and never found. The clean-up team were reported to have suffered from radiation sickness, resulting in a high incidence of cancer.

Qaanaaq was a very welcoming place and was a hive of activity. The annual supply ships had just arrived and cargo was being unloaded onto lighters for transport to shore. The ships carry their own lighters in Greenland (lighters are small shallow-draft, barge-like vessels, used to discharge cargo when no deep-water harbour is available).

Without the protection of a natural harbour, the lighters were discharging their cargo on the beach with the protection of a small breakwater that covers at half tide.

Also at anchor offshore was the Greenpeace ship *Arctic Sunrise,* and *Turmoil,* a motor yacht built in the style and sea-keeping abilities of a North Sea trawler.

The *Politi* (police) couldn't have been more helpful. In their four-wheel drive jeep they drove us around, showing us the laundry house and then bringing us for coffee in the local hotel. There we met a group of Danish geologists, waiting for supplies and better weather for their fieldwork.

That evening we had showers in the community hall – and thus cleaned and inspired we sang and played a few tunes later for some of the locals. An old man performed one of their drum-dance stories. Interestingly, the local people used their Inuit first names unlike in south Greenland where they all have Christian names. The forklift trucks worked all night on the beach bringing the cargo up from the tidal area. At this latitude in summer there is 24-hour daylight. Children played on the beach all night, unconcerned despite the cold rain that fell. June is known locally as 'the month when no one sleeps'.

Next day the wind increased to force 6. We lay at anchor fending off the occasional ice floes that drifted down on us. A second ship arrived and was unloading its cargo in difficult conditions. A new fire engine being delivered was nearly lost when a strong gust of wind blew the lighter onto the breakwater; luckily it was hauled off and taken back to the ship to await better weather.

We were invited aboard the Greenpeace ship *Arctic Sunrise* for dinner and what they called a

The Greenpeace ship, Arctic Sunrise.

'limited bar'; I'm not sure what the limit was – perhaps we raised it upwards with the bottles of Irish whiskey we brought aboard as appetisers. They showed us around their vessel, told us of their campaign, listened to our songs, and joined in the chorus. A particular line in the 'Greenland Whale Fishery' raised a rousing cheer: 'and we did not catch that whale, brave boys, and we did not catch that whale.' What a night we had with those cheerful, dedicated people.

There was a certain ambivalence towards Greenpeace locally because of Greenpeace's opposition to whaling and to the US 'star wars' air base. Many local people are employed in the air base. The natives take a small number of whales each year. Nevertheless, the Greenlanders were friendly towards the *Arctic Sunrise* crew. Greenpeace now recognise that the traditional Inuit subsistence hunting practices have minimal effect on the whale population and have dropped their earlier opposition.

Next day we got a permit from the Qaanaaq community which allowed us take a trip up Inglefjord where sightings of Narwhal were 'guaranteed'. This permit specified that sail only be used. Search as we might, we failed to get a single sighting. Narwhal is a medium-sized whale found in Arctic waters. The species not only lacks a dorsal fin but the male Narwhal has a distinguishing feature unique in the world of whales: a tooth that grows into a long, spiral tusk that may reach 9 feet. Narwhals have a cylindrical body, with a blunt head and small mouth. Males average about 16 feet in length; females about 13 feet.

As we settled down to living together in our snug confined cabin, we were all aware that everyone needs their own exclusive space, no matter how small that may be. In our case everyone had their own berth with storage cupboards alongside. The space underneath each berth was filled with food supplies, sufficient for at least two seasons in the Arctic. In fact, we carried over two tonnes of food. We had a vast quantity of porridge; Paddy Barry specialised in cooking our breakfast and his porridge recipe included honey and raisins. On this diet alone, we could thrive for years.

We were blessed in having good cooks with us – Michael, Gary, Tom and Rory – each of whom could produce a gourmet meal no matter how far we were from land. For a good standby meal in times of heavy weather, we had canned chicken and mushroom pies, and steak and kidney pies. Eight tins were opened and placed in the Dickinson oven for 30 minutes to produce a delicious meal straight from the tin. Rory's speciality was a wonderful concoction of chopped ham, pineapple and rice curry. Our diet included pasta in all its forms and when possible we bought fresh fish and caribou. We enjoyed fresh bread daily, baked using Odlums bread mix. Should we have to abandon ship, we carried 200 army, 24-hour ration packs, each pack containing the food needed for a day's march across the tundra.

At the beginning, several people predicted dire conflicts between the 'three sea captains' – myself, Paddy and Michael – all of whom have captained their own boats and have strong wills.

While there may have been some differences of opinion on the best way to achieve our goal we all had the same interest in completing the voyage. The phrase, 'be reasonable, do it my way', usually sorted out problems. The evening music sessions, in which we all joined, were a great asset in team bonding.

We spoke briefly with Gary Comer, owner of *Turmoil*, who also planned an attempt on the transit of the North West Passage. We agreed to keep in radio contact. The ice reports were showing improving conditions on the southern side of Lancaster Sound.

It was time to be on our way.

6

QAANAAQ TO
CAMBRIDGE BAY

We sailed south-westwards towards Devon Island, Canada, to the north of Lancaster Sound, first in sunshine, and later in dense fog. Using radar and depth sounder, we found our way into Coburg Island where we anchored in 3 metres depth in a sheltered bay. The Canadian and the new Nunavut flags were raised and a celebratory bottle of Canadian whiskey was opened. The new Canadian territory of Nunavut was created in 1999 giving the indigenous people a voice in the territory's evolution.

Next day, after a run ashore, we were on our way again in better conditions down outside Jones sound, then through light ice and fog, to the eastward of Devon Island, to Cape Sherard, the entrance to Lancaster Sound. We rounded the Cape at 04.00 on Tuesday 7 August in good visibility, no ice to be seen and the sun shining on the mountain tops. All was well in our small world, as we continued westward, noting the names on the charts of famous headlands and bays, wondering why Cape Joy is so called.

The notes on the charts say 'compass useless', which was quite true. The compass card appeared lazy, unreliable and slow to move as we were now near the magnetic north pole. Sometimes the compass card spun uncontrollably. The autopilot was also disabled, as it needed input from its

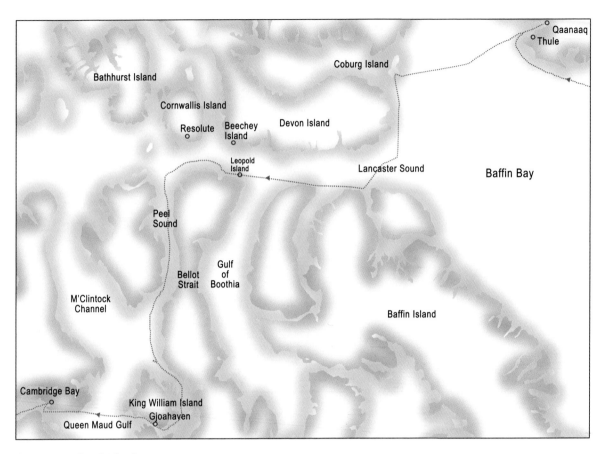

Qaanaaq to Cambridge Bay.

magnetic compass. As we were steering by hand, and keeping a good look out, this was not a problem at the moment. We plotted our GPS position on the chart to check our track.

We spoke with a Canadian icebreaker, *Louis St Lauren*, eastbound from Resolute. Her ice pilot was most helpful. They had broken through 7/10 pack ice to get out of Resolute and met an area of 7/10 ice near where we were heading. They advised us to try to skirt it to the south. This agreed with our ice chart information.

Having diverted to the south shore of Lancaster Sound, by evening we were again into heavy ice and fog. Paddy and Frank climbed the mast, and from their look-out position on the spreaders, they would point out leads. The only problem with this arrangement was, I discovered, that conflicting instructions tended to be given. While Paddy was instructing me to steer to port, Frank would recommend starboard, and the man at the bow might be telling me go straight ahead! I learned to limit my lookouts aloft to one man only at a time to indicate the direction to steer. We forced our way through leads, occasionally being stopped by heavier ice (a lead is an open fissure through the ice field).

The technique we used to get through heavier ice was to place a man aloft on the mast spreaders to seek out a lead going in the right direction. *Northabout* would then carefully push its way through until stopped by a floe in its path. To move the floe aside, we increased the engine revs driving the bow against the floe. We usually also had to apply pressure with our ice poles to force the floe aside. These ice poles are timber poles about 12 feet long. With our ice poles pushing floes aside and the engine driving, we would gradually move quite

We met the eastbound Canadian ice-breaker, Louis St Lauren.

large floes and go forward to the next obstacle, begin the process all over again. If the ice didn't yield, we had to reverse back as far as possible and have another try, sometimes in another lead.

To prevent damage to the rudder while reversing, *Northabout* has a strong alloy 'fin' directly behind the rudder, extending well below the waterline. We found that this fin worked very successfully as we rammed the ice behind to make more room to turn.

We continued to make slow progress westward, the ice getting heavier all the time. We banged into floes, broke through some and bounced off others. *Northabout's* bow was carefully designed to ride up on to floating ice thereby absorbing the shock that would have occurred had it hit ice head on. After impact the ice would either break and move aside, or *Northabout* would slide back down again to have another go. Without the unique features of the raised ice-breaker bow and the rudder fin, we would be vulnerable to serious damage. Great credit must go to the designer of this unique vessel.

By the approach of midnight on Wednesday 8 August no further progress could be made. We were completely surrounded by ice, with no apparent way out. There was no choice but to anchor to the ice and await developments.

John went filming on the ice and we had Terry beside him with shotgun on bear watch, while Kevin and Michael tried their luck fishing. In my off-watch spell I read an Arctic survival book, which amongst many useful tips has this gem: 'Your luck runs out just when you need it most.'

It is said that Arctic travel is all about waiting; the ice is constantly moving, sometimes for the worse, sometimes for the better. Patience is an Arctic virtue. The GPS indicated we were drifting eastwards with the ice, losing the miles we had struggled so hard to gain.

As the ice tightened its grip around us, the unwelcome thought of being frozen-in so early in the trip crossed my mind. I could feel the silent tension below as others had the same thought but nobody voiced it. They kept their worst fears to themselves.

By morning all had changed. At 9am we broke free of the ice, the leads opened up gradually

From top left: Northabout *beset in ice; John filming on the ice; Terry on bear watch*.

and soon we got underway again, relieved to be moving, but not knowing when the ice would again close in on us. With the northern side of Lancaster Sound still choked with $^9/_{10}$ ice, we were forced to abandon our plan to visit Beechey Island to see the site where Franklin's two ships spent their first winter and where three of Franklin's crew are buried. Instead we set our course for Port Leopold on the south side of Lancaster Sound.

As we approached Port Leopold it was apparent the bay was blocked with ice, making it impossible to land. However, sailing onwards to the west side of the peninsula, we saw Rhodo Bay was ice free. It was always difficult for us to make the choice between our desire to push on or alternatively to spend some time exploring and sightseeing. While we knew we must take advantage of the short window of opportunity for Arctic travel, there would be little point in rushing through without seeing anything. We therefore decided to land, having anchored in 4 metres depth at 03.30 am with the sun still shining in the northern horizon. A hike of four miles across the gravel peninsula took us back to Port Leopold. In the bay, a pod of white Beluga whales were cavorting and swimming, obviously enjoying themselves. In size and appearance, they are rather similar to dolphins, apart from their white colour.

On the shore a stone hut lay abandoned and empty and a cairn built nearby had a plaque dated 1974 commemorating past explorers who gave their lives so gallantly. The real find of the day was an inscribed rock with the inscription 'E.I. 1849', presumably engraved by the crew of the *Enterprise* and *Investigator* who wintered here in 1848-49 under the command of James Clark Ross, on the first of many searches for Franklin.

In this bleak place we accidentally disturbed a couple asleep in their tent. They were combining kayaking with bird-watching in the area and were hoping to make the crossing to Leopold Island with suitable weather. We were amazed to find such enthusiastic people in so remote a spot.

In the afternoon, under full sail, we moved towards Peel Sound 50 miles distant, in high spirits, with sunny skies. According to all our research, Peel Sound is the bottleneck and choke point of our route. In some years the ice never breaks up or clears. Historically this has been the barrier to the North West Passage.

We approached the entrance to Peel Sound – Limestone Island – and then past Granite Point, and sailed south into the Sound where the water was unbelievably ice free, wondering how long our good luck would last. The only ice visible was some loose brash. We all kept silent in case our luck should change for the worse. A fair wind helped our progress now and we sailed 'goose winged' down the strait; with the genoa poled out to port and the mainsail to starboard, to take advantage of the wind from astern.

Left to right: *Sunset near Port Leopold; Frank, Michael and Paddy on the rock bearing the inscription 'EI 1849' referring to the* Enterprise *and* Investigator *that overwintered in the area.*

Bellot Strait on our port side was choked with ice. Pemmican Rock in the entrance, mentioned in so many explorers' accounts, lay obscured by hummocked floes; we had hoped to see this landmark. As we continued on our way we soon entered bands of loose ice. Though these slowed our speed, we continued to make progress.

On Saturday 11 August, a new event occurred; the sun dipped below the horizon for the first time for months and returned two and a half hours later.

By evening we entered James Ross Strait and built a cairn on Cape Victoria. We placed a message in a whiskey bottle (empty, of course) and took photographs of Donk, Terry's toy donkey mascot who travels on all his trips – Terry photographed him in all the exotic places visited. We found traces of hunter's campsites – stone circles to hold their tents in position – and saw caribou nearby. A plane flew low overhead, which we recognised as *Turmoil*'s on an ice reconnaissance mission.

Shortly after leaving on Sunday morning, despite careful navigation, we ran aground on a sand-bank about one mile offshore. Luckily the weather was calm and the sea flat. Thanks to the retractable centreboard, which we raised, we were soon off the bank, relieved to be underway again. The chart shows many shoals in this area but as the sand is shifted by ice during winter, charted depths may not be accurate. In any case, only the main channel is charted in these waters.

James Ross Strait is narrow and shallow. We wound our way through, in near-perfect conditions,

Sunset at Leopold Island.

The crew and 'Donk' at the cairn we built in Cape Victoria.

looking for an island shown PA (position approximate) on our chart. When seen, it was close abeam, a group of rocky fangs barely visible over water, a half mile off its reported position.

We proceeded down the east coast of King William Island, close to Matty Island where Amundsen's *Gjoa* went aground and was nearly lost. Ballast had been removed from *Gjoa* and provisions sacrificed to refloat her. *Gjoa* had another potentially disastrous incident when fire broke out near the petrol tanks; fortunately it was extinguished before the tanks exploded.

As we approached Gjoahaven along the route described by Amundsen, we again touched bottom, though we quickly got off by raising the centreboard. I was reminded once again about the shifting sands of the Arctic.

In Gjoahaven Bay we anchored off and went ashore by dinghy. We later moored *Northabout* at the small pier to take on supplies.

The Royal Canadian Mounted Police (RCMP), Todd and Christine, welcomed us, the first boat to visit that year. We made our formal entry to Canada, with minimum difficulty. The police couldn't be more helpful; we were expected here, of course. Paddy had been in communication with the Canadian authorities in advance and had dealt with all queries raised, in particular that we were not carriers of foot and mouth disease.

Kevin with a heroic sculpture of Amundsen in Gjoahaven. Two similar sculptures exist, one in Nome, Alaska, and one in Tromso, Norway.

The RCMP allowed us the use of their showers and washing machines, and later took us for a drive around the settlement. The most prominent feature in the settlement is the Distant Early Warning (DEW) station radome just outside the town. These remotely controlled stations were built by the American and Canadian governments during the Cold War to give early warning of approaching missiles, and they are located at centres approximately every 300 miles along the North West Passage.

On *Northabout* there was work to be done; the rigging needed adjustment, engine oil and filters had to be changed and the tanks refilled. Gearóid and I got on with the work, while Paddy, Michael and Frank were entertaining the locals in the community centre. They, in retaliation, were entertained by an interminably long drum dance.

Amundsen overwintered in this bay in 1904 and 1905. From his description of the harbour the topography has changed considerably since that time. The river where he laid up *Gjoa* has now silted up. Amundsen set up shore stations for scientific research, particularly the study of the earth's magnetic field. During the Norwegians' visit more and more natives settled in the area, which eventually developed in to the small town of today. The native Netsilik Eskimos (or Inuit as they prefer) traded with the Norwegians and visited *Gjoa*. Amundsen forbade his crew to form liaisons with the native women, though he seemed to have excepted himself from this rule. I met a hunter who introduced himself as Paul Amundsen, claiming to be a direct descendant and he was certainly the image of the great explorer.

Amundsen learned to live like the natives in the harsh winter climate, learning dog-handling skills, sledge driving and adopting the native fur clothing. This, I believe, was the reason why he was successful in the race to the South Pole, where unfortunately the less experienced Scott and his four companions perished.

Michael Brogan writes:

Muskox – Ovibos Oschatus *or* Umingmak *in Inuktitut.*

To see a Muskox is to look back into prehistoric times. These animals are creatures of the last ice age. They are bulky animals with a prominent shoulder hump, a long thick coat of hair and low curving horns that meet in a heavy boss across the forehead. The dark brown outer coat of hair covers a thick layer of fine wool known as quivit *which is regarded as the best natural fibre in terms of insulation. The muskox is almost impervious to low temperatures.*

Muskoxen are classified with sheep and goats in the Bovidae *family and live in small family groups of eight to fourteen animals. The adults will charge a person especially if their calves are threatened. On Victoria Island we were advised to run in circles if charged. Apparently muskox cannot turn quickly. Thankfully we did not have to put this theory to the test although we did get close to some animals.*

An adult bull stands 140 to 150 cm at the shoulder and weighs 325 to 400 kg. Prior to the arrival of the Europeans in North America muskoxen roamed the tundra in great numbers. In the last century their number were greatly reduced by fur traders and whalers. About 23,000 muskox hides were harvested from the North American tundra between 1860 and 1915. By 1915 estimates of the numbers remaining on the tundra were in the order of 450 to 500 animals. The ▶

A muskox.

Canadian government gave them total protection from hunting in 1917 except for indigenous people at risk of starvation. Killing of muskoxen was totally prohibited in 1924 in the North West Territories. From the mid 1960s the population in Canada has exploded and the present number is estimated at 120,000 animals.

Muskox have recently been introduced into regions that have not seen them for decades including Alaska, Greenland, Norway, Svalbard, Wrangle Island and the Taymyr Peninsula in Russia where the herd of 30 animals introduced in 1975 has now risen to 2,500 animals.

Our new friends in *MV Turmoil* arrived later and invited us aboard for dinner. A visit to a mega-yacht is an eye-opening experience, particularly for those of us accustomed to the frugal comforts of *Northabout*. On arrival, we were warmly greeted and given moccasins to wear aboard. The entry through the polished stainless steel and pristine white engine room was impressive and a foretaste of the quality and the craftsmanship aboard this fine craft. Nevertheless, despite the fine finishes, *Turmoil* is not a luxury toy; it is a working expedition boat, with voyages to far distant places on the globe from the Amazon to Kamchatka and Japan. The owner, Gary Comer and his wife Francie, were the perfect hosts. We brought along a couple of bottles of Irish whiskey, a small addition to

Gary Comer's megayacht Turmoil, *which was also attempting the North West Passage.*

Above: *Inukshuk (singular), meaning 'likeness of a person' in Inuktitut (the Inuit language), is a stone figure made by the Inuit. The plural is inuksuit. The Inuit make inuksuit in different forms and for different purposes: to show directions to travellers, to warn of impending danger, to mark a place of respect or to act as helpers in the hunting of caribou. Similar stone figures were made all over the world in ancient times but the Arctic is one of the few places where they still stand. An Inukshuk can be small or large, a single rock, several rocks balanced on each other, round boulders or flat. Inuit tradition forbids the destruction of inuksuit.*

Right: *A skull found at Todd Island, undoubtedly a remnant of the Franklin expedition.*

Turmoil's excellent cellar, which helped to get the sing-song going. An excellent meal was laid on and it was early morning before we departed singing 'goodnight Irene' to the cheering waves of *Turmoil's* crew on the upper deck.

Our departure was not as early as planned in the morning. *Turmoil* had departed an hour earlier than us – no bad heads amongst that professional crew! We got underway and sailed to Todd Island. In Gjoahaven, John had been given a 'Treasure Island' hand-drawn chart of the island, indicating where the skeletons of some of Franklin's crew might be found. We anchored, dinghied

Paddy trying on traditional fur clothing in Gjoahaven.

ashore, and fanned out across the island. Sure enough, we found a bleached skull amid the rocks, almost certainly from Franklin's era. Not wishing to disturb the scene we left everything as we found it.

One could almost feel the anguish of this sailor as he struggled across this barren landscape trying to make his way to sanctuary. Somewhere to the north of here Franklin's ships were beset in the ice and eventually sank. The crew, or what remained of them, struggled unsuccessfully to reach Backs Fish River where aid might be found.

Turmoil's floatplane flew low overhead waggling wings, as if mocking us for our excesses of the previous night.

Soon we were on our way, down Simpson Strait and into Queen Maud Gulf. This involved tricky navigation in the narrow rocky channels as we made our way to the town of Cambridge Bay on Victoria Island, 250 miles away. The wind rose during the night to force 8, right on the bow, slowing our speed down to 2 knots in the bumpy seas. The night was pitch black. As progress was virtually nil, we sought shelter overnight in Secchi Bay. By mid-morning the wind had eased and we got underway again, and without further incident we arrived in Cambridge Bay where we tied alongside the jetty on Thursday 16 August.

Cambridge Bay (Ikaluktutiak) is a small town on the south-east coast of Victoria Island. The people of the area are referred to as 'Copper Eskimos' since they made a variety of implements from native copper. The settlement is a transport and supply centre for all the DEW Line sites in the area. All supplies and services are very expensive here, as everywhere in the Arctic, because of the high cost of transporting goods.

The weather forced us to extend our planned one-day stopover. We were stormbound for four days. The gale blew and blew, first from the west and then increased to 40 knots from the north west. The

The remains in Cambridge Bay of Amundsen's vessel, Maud, *in which he sailed the North East Passage.* Maud *was later sold to the Hudson Bay Company and named* Baymaud.

seas were banging *Northabout* against the jetty and damaging her stanchions, so we moved and anchored three miles up the west bay. Though there was reasonable shelter in the bay, the wind was now so strong that we laid out a second heavy anchor for security. We returned to the jetty later the next evening when the wind had eased. Raising the 90lb anchor and chain took a long time and much effort.

We met some great people ashore: Pat who ran the power plant, Andy an electrical contractor and Wilf a general contractor. The town is 'dry', meaning alcohol free, as decided by the community. The town has a modern look about it; most of the buildings look fairly new and all are well insulated, though we felt the temperature inside most buildings was too hot.

To avoid melting the permafrost and damaging the foundations, all buildings are raised up on supports to keep the warm floor away from the ground. Some of the more modern buildings have taken the concept even further; the supports incorporate screw jacks; as the building settles the jacks are adjusted to keep the floor level.

Kevin tried his hand at fishing and succeeded in landing an Arctic char, which made a delicious change to our diet of tinned food.

The wreck of *Maud* lay awash in the bay. This was the vessel in which Amundsen sailed the North East Passage and attempted to drift in the ice to the North Pole. The four North Pole expeditions bankrupted him, forcing the sale of *Maud* to satisfy his creditors. The Hudson Bay Company purchased her in 1926 and re-named her *Baymaud* for use as an Arctic supply vessel. *Baymaud* sank at her moorings here in 1931. Though wrecked, she did not altogether die; the RCMP vessel *St Roch*, in which Captain Larsen later transitted the North West Passage, was modelled on the lines of *Baymaud*.

Terry Irvine had to leave us at this time to return to work. With the help of Wilf, he succeeded in getting a very reasonably-priced fare to Edmonton. Donk, Terry's mascot, was left with us to complete the voyage.

While we were in Cambridge Bay, we spoke via radio with Philip Walsh, captain of *Turmoil*; they had left Cambridge Bay before we arrived. As they were travelling at 22 knots compared with our 6.5 knots, we assumed it unlikely that we would see them again. However, their head start was useful to us as Philip reported very heavy ice at Cape Parry. We hoped we could get through the next ice barrier and at least get to Tuktoyaktuk on the Mackenzie River that year.

The wind at this stage had moderated to a reasonable 20 knots as we set sail from Cambridge Bay for the next part of the journey.

7

CAMBRIDGE BAY TO TUKTOYUKTUK

On Sunday morning, 19 August, we left Cambridge Bay with gifts of frozen Arctic char and cheerful shouts of 'may the leads open before you, and 'may the water be deeper than your keel'.

Our next destination was Tuktoyuktuk (known locally as Tuk), 650 miles ahead. The wind was still quite strong but once we got going and faced into the sea it wasn't a problem. The apparent wind in the harbour always seems worse than it actually is once one gets underway.

As we sailed down Dease Strait and into Coronation Gulf, conditions were good; ice-free seas, wind easing, and later, flat calm seas with the sun in the west.

On Monday morning we made radio contact with the coastguard vessel *Henry Larson* to ask about ice conditions at Cape Parry. They reported conditions were not good; ⁶/₁₀ to ⁹/₁₀ ice but, they suggested, there might be a shore lead. Interestingly, they told us that Peel Sound, safely behind us, was by now completely blocked with ice. Good timing on our part!

At 10am in Coronation Gulf, Franklin's Turnagain Point was abeam. Franklin named this point as the furthest east of his first overland expedition of 1819-21. On their return journey from this expedition the explorers suffered great hardships and starvation, surviving on lichen and ultimately eating their boots. Franklin became known throughout England as 'The man who ate his boots'.

On Tuesday afternoon we entered Dolphin and Union Strait. Conditions were still good, with flat seas, good visibility, no ice, and travelling at a speed of 6.8 knots.

By late evening we encountered some loose ice, which reduced our speed to a still respectable 5 knots. We collected some ice from an iceberg to melt for fresh water. The news was also good from Brendan, who sent the latest ice chart via HF radio to our laptop computer. It showed generally $^2/_{10}$ ice cover with a band of $^7/_{10}$ ice cover on the west side of Darnley Bay.

However, at midnight a band of $^9/_{10}$ ice was in sight. We diverted south-west into the bay to skirt it and dodged the frequent growlers. By morning, we had worked our way through $^2/_{10}$ ice with 11 miles to go to Cape Parry. All day long we continued dodging the growlers and forcing our way through the ice and by midnight Cape Parry was astern. A major objective, one that caused us much apprehension on this part of the journey, was achieved.

The direct route to Cape Bathurst was 80 miles as the crow flies; unfortunately, the direct route was blocked with impassable ice. To avoid it we diverted along the shore into Franklin Bay, more than doubling the distance to be travelled but avoiding the heavy ice. A strong current helped to maintain a speed of 9 knots, and by morning we were in ice-free water at last. Continuing our long diversion around the bay, by 10.30 in the evening the smoking hills were abeam. The smoking hills

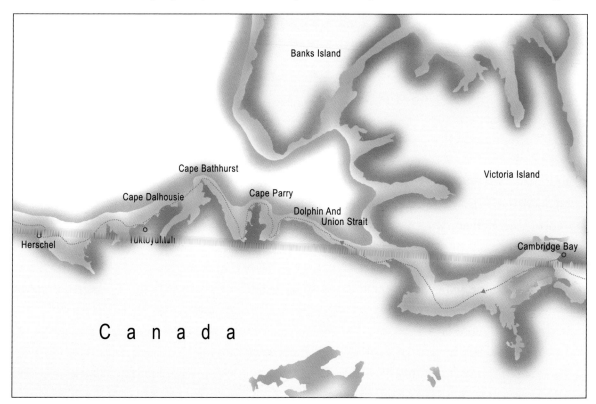

Cambridge Bay to Herschel Island.

Clockwise from top left: *oil drilling rigs; sailing goose winged; DEW Station.*

were noted by early explorers. The smoke comes from coal deposits burning underground. Later, a very dense fog descended, reducing visibility to virtually nil.

On Sunday afternoon we rounded Cape Bathurst and Baillie Islands still in fog, and plotted the final leg to Tuktoyuktuk – a distance of 95 miles. We sailed past oil rigs, some of them now derelict. To drill for oil in these shallow waters, artificial islands were created on which the drilling rigs were set up. When the rigs were removed the islands remained, left to erode over time. A good lookout is needed to avoid them, as they may be semi-submerged. Another navigation hazard are the 'pingos', underwater mounds pushed upwards by ice and water pressure.

At mid morning we moored at the NTCC jetty in Tuktoyuktuk, on the mighty Mackenzie River – another milestone achieved. We now dared to hope that we might succeed in our attempt on the North West Passage in one season.

Tuktoyuktuk serves as a supply and service station to the Arctic communities, and in the 1970s and 1980s was a boomtown because of oil and gas exploration in the nearby Beaufort Sea area. The boom times are over as the oil companies moved on, leaving Tuk with a ghost town appearance, many of the buildings neglected and derelict.

Supplies are delivered by barge down the Mackenzie River to Tuk for trans-shipment in sea-going barges which are towed up to six at a time to the isolated communities and DEW stations.

Winter transportation is done on ice roads. When the sea freezes to about 7 feet in ice-thickness, a route is marked and levelled, along which a Cat D8 bulldozer will pull a 'cat-train' of sledges, including a 'sleeping-car', for the workers and drivers.

We topped up our diesel tanks, while Frank manufactured a pin for the autopilot on Wilson Adey's lathe. Wilson,

whom we had just met, treated us as if we were old friends and gave us the free run of his machine shop. Gearóid, with his expertise in electronics, and I, spent a long time investigating a mysterious fault in the HF radio. We eventually traced the problem to a loose connection inside the Antenna Tuning Unit (ATU). Unfortunately, because of the fault in the ATU, the radio was damaged. We fitted the spare radio and all was in working order again.

Later, the local RCMP invited us to a barbecue at their home and allowed us use of their showers. In return, we sang for our supper.

Top: Northabout *sailing through open leads in the evening sunlight.* Above: *Wilson Adley and Frank in Tuktoyuktuk, with the newly-machined replacement pin for the autopilot.*

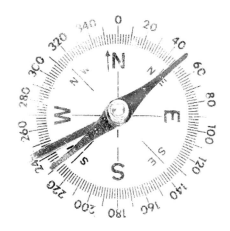

8

TUKTOYUKTUK
TO NOME

With the completion of the North West Passage so tantalisingly close, we cast off our mooring lines at first light on Saturday morning, 25 August, bound towards Point Barrow, 450 miles away. Barrow was discovered by Europeans in 1825 and Frederick William Beechey named it after Sir John Barrow of the British Admiralty.

The first 120 miles across Mackenzie Bay was a delight. In a following wind our headsails were 'goose winged', a trade wind rig seldom set in the cold Arctic.

Michael cooked a breakfast of caribou stew and dinner was caribou shank à la Tuk. It was delicious.

Before we left Tuktoyuktuk we fully investigated the faulty autopilot. We had assumed the problems we had been having were caused by our proximity to the north magnetic pole but now that we were less influenced by the polar anomaly, it became clear we had other problems. Gearoid, our electronics man, made several expensive telephone calls to the manufacturers in England. As their technician guided him through a series of tests, our worst fears were confirmed: it was dead! 'Drop it into your local agent for service' was the final helpful suggestion. As the nearest agent was over 2,000 miles away, this wasn't much help.

While we had a full crew, the loss of the autopilot was not a serious issue; in the Arctic waters we were hand steering in any case. Once around Point Barrow and into more open seas, the autopilot would have helped relieve the tedium of being at the helm constantly.

By evening we sailed into shallow water near Pullen Island with drizzle and choppy seas making conditions miserable and uncomfortable.

When Amundsen was in *Gjoa* in 1906 he met heavy ice in this area and was forced to sail close to the shore, eventually becoming beset in the ice at King Point. During the winter here one of his crew, Wiik, died unexpectedly after suffering for a few days with pain in his right side. He was buried ashore later on 9 May. As there was no hope of moving *Gjoa* until the following year's break up, Roald Amundsen took an arduous inland journey over the mountains by dog sled to the telegraph office at Eagle City on the Yukon River. Here he was able to announce to the outside world that he had completed the first transit of the North West Passage. He waited there for two months to receive mail from home and then returned to *Gjoa* with letters for his news-starved crew.

Quite a few ships were in the vicinity during our visit; we spoke on VHF radio with *Geko Snapper* doing a seismic survey, and with an NTCL tug off the starboard bow. They reported a sighting of bowhead whales, and gave us the latitude and longitude of where they were seen. Mike sighted two bowhead whales later.

Northabout *crew with a park ranger at the former whaling and trading station on Herschel island.*

In darkness and dense fog we approached Herschel Island, avoiding a band of ice near Collison Head. With Michael's navigational skill and the aid of radar and depth-sounder, we cautiously entered Pauline Cove in Thetis Bay and anchored for the night. In the morning we went ashore by dinghy and met Ricky and Frank, the rangers in charge of Herschel Island Territorial Park.

They gave us a tour of part of the island, which was formerly the base for the American whaling fleet. Frank told us some of his grandfather's stories and how the 2,000 members of the indigenous population of the region were practically wiped out by white man's diseases, to which they had no immunity. Frank's grandfather had told him 'when the local people died off, the whalers brought in other natives from outside to do the work for them, all for a few guns, alcohol and trinkets. The white man came in woman's black clothes (soutane). Ten years later we had the Book, the Bible, and they had the land.' As in other parts of the world, religion gets the blame for causing strife.

Herschel Island, or Qikiqtaruk as it is known in the Inuvialuit language, is a land 'where it is good to live' according to Nuligak, an Inuvialuit hunter. It has a deep sheltered harbour where the whaling fleet could winter in safety. Its shores are littered with driftwood and it has a covering of tough grass, with plentiful wildlife.

The distance from Herschel to Point Barrow was 400 miles. The latest ice charts showed a 50-mile wide band of ice along Demarcation Point, then an ice-free area beyond. In the open Beaufort Sea we would be exposed to drifting polar pack ice and no longer sheltered from the north by the islands. Wind-blown ice drifts slightly to the right of the true wind direction (in the northern hemisphere). This is caused by the Coriolis effect (the same force that causes water exiting a bath to rotate). Therefore, with the easterly wind now blowing, the ice should be moving out from the shore, giving a clear passage to Point Barrow.

As we left Herschel Island we saw a polar bear on the shore, which took fright and ran up a seemingly impossibly steep cliff and disappeared out of sight. Up to then I thought that if I was unlucky enough to encounter a bear on land, I would be able to outrun such an obviously heavy and cumbersome animal. I now know, having seen its strength and agility, that it would be impossible to out-manoeuvre a polar bear.

Under sail and engine, we made good progress in ice-free conditions, though with dense fog. On Sunday 26 August, as we approached Demarcation Point, longitude 141 degrees west, we had a flag-raising ceremony. The Maple Leaf was lowered, and the Stars and Stripes hoisted as we entered Alaskan waters. A tot was issued to celebrate the event.

How is it that every time one celebrates such an event things go horribly wrong? Soon, heavy ice appeared and as we weaved through leads we crossed and re-crossed the border many times. We moved closer inshore, hoping to avoid the worst of the ice, and with no improvement in sight, decided to anchor for a while in Demarcation Bay. As we neared the narrow entrance, the gearbox emitted loud squealing sounds. The engine was stopped immediately and the sails were raised. Through the ice we slowly sailed into the bay and, when safely anchored, I examined the gearbox.

At Demarkation Bay, 141 degrees west, we cross the border line between Canada and Alaska. The maple leaf of Canada is lowered and the stars and stripes of the USA is hoisted.

All kinds of thoughts entered my mind; were we stuck here for the winter or would it be possible to sail through ice-strewn seas to civilisation?

The problem appeared to be a hydraulic oil leak somewhere in the gearbox. The dipstick indicated low oil level, in fact no oil on the dipstick at all. The oil was topped up, and the engine started. To our great joy the gears engaged and no damage was apparent. The puzzle remained; where had the oil gone, as there was no obvious leak and no sign of oil in the bilges. For the rest of the trip the gearbox continually lost oil and was topped up daily. Later we found the source of the leak – oil was seeping through gaskets, the lost oil accumulating under the engine.

After seven hours' rest, we got underway again, still in dense fog with visibility less than 500 metres. We closely followed the coast, keeping between the shingle shore and the grounded floes outside. The floes generally run aground in about 3 metres depth.

With centreboard raised, *Northabout* draws about 1.4 metres. We were able to maintain our progress, though frequently touching bottom.

On Tuesday 28 August we ran hard aground; no amount of engine revving or pushing with poles could get us off. By offloading most of the crew into the dinghy to lighten ship, we succeeded eventually in winching her off using an anchor set in deeper water.

By evening Maguire Islands were abeam. This was our coldest day so far; we were sailing through freezing fog and ice formed on the shrouds and on the running rigging. Beards and eyebrows collected ice too, as our breath condensed and froze. The helmsman was dodging icicles falling from the rigging. Kevin said that this was a two-hat day! In icy conditions, he wore his two hats. After midnight, Barter Island was abeam to port, though visible on radar only.

We decided to take the inside route, a passage inside the low-lying sand banks. We entered at Challenge entrance and made our way past the barely-visible oil drilling rigs in Prudhoe Bay and onwards towards Cape Halkett. Ice had now formed on the deck, the sails and the rigging. The weather forecast was not good; north-east wind rising to 20 knots, later increasing to 30 knots. Despite the cold and adverse conditions we pushed on, every watch getting us nearer to Barrow.

We crossed Harrison Bay and forced our way through ice off Cape Halkett. By evening the distance to Point Barrow was reduced to 85 miles.

Early next morning, 30 August, in a lively rising wind we rounded Point Barrow. Ashore, through the light fog, we could see people driving their jeeps. I suspect they were wondering what kind of madmen would be out sailing in such wild conditions. The seas at this stage were breaking, making life on board very uncomfortable.

At 71.235 degrees north, Barrow Cape is the most northerly point of Alaska. It marks the end of the North West Passage, our goal for the past three months and our dream for many years.

Our transit time through the North West Passage was faster than most previous attempts. *Northabout* entered Lancaster Sound on 7 August and rounded Point Barrow on 30 August, a record time of 24 days.

We round Point Barrow in fog and heavy seas. This marks the end of the North West Passage but not the end of our voyage.

Monument to celebrate the three lucky Swedish men who discovered gold in Nome.

We all looked forward to a celebratory breakfast ashore in Barrow and to visit Alaska's most northerly community, the native Inupiat whalers, made famous by Charles Brower's book, *Fifty Years Below Zero*. Brower, a New York sailor, came to Barrow in 1885 aged 22, and formed a whale hunting and trading station. He lived there for the next 55 years, successfully trading and became known as 'The King of the Arctic'.

Landing for us proved impossible; the seas were too high and dangerous to anchor. Instead, we opted for a tot of whiskey and three cheers for the fine team!

The breakfast ashore had to wait while we travelled another 600 miles, to the gold-mining town of Nome. In a gale from astern we flew through the Chukchi Sea and through the Bering Sea, passing the unseen Diamedes Islands on our starboard, and we finally entered into the marina in the harbour of Nome.

The customs officer, when he finally appeared after his weekend away, was not impressed with our achievement. He claimed (rightly) that our documentation was incorrect and that we were liable to a fine of $15,000 each and confiscation of the boat. The problem was that while we all had valid visa waivers to enter the USA, this waiver only applies when entering by regular airline or passenger ferry, and does not apply to persons entering by private yacht. The US embassy in Dublin didn't make that point to us.

After long-distance telephone discussions with officials in Anchorage, we were welcomed to the Land of the Free.

Nome, that evocative sounding name, held a fascination for me, maybe because of Robert Service's poems of the 'Men who moil for gold' or the hit song of my youth – Johnny Horton's 'North to Alaska'. I was determined to try my luck at gold panning.

The town of Nome was established during the gold rush of 1898 when gold was discovered in Anvil Creek, and the next year in the beach sand. The mother lode was never found, only placer gold (flakes eroded and carried in the sand). Today, Nome still has the appearance of a frontier town (actually called a city, though the population is a mere 3,600). The people we met were all larger than life, and full of the joys. Many women migrate to Alaska from the

Northabout *is lifted out and laid-up ashore in Nome.*

'Lower 48' seeking their fortune or to meet the man of their dreams. One disillusioned young woman told me, 'The odds are good, but the goods are odd'!

Anne Millbrook of the *Nome Nugget* (the oldest newspaper in Alaska) interviewed us and wrote an article for the paper. Anne later took us gold prospecting on the beach. With shovels and pans, we swirled the sand like the old timers and picked out the gold with tweezers. Yes, there is lots of gold in the sand still, and the excitement of finding big nuggets keeps a group of prospectors working on the beach, always hopeful of finding the mother lode. Gold is there for anyone that wants to pick it up – it depends on one's luck. My afternoon's panning yielded about $5, hardly a fortune, but one never knows; the next pan might be full of nuggets.

At this stage most of the crew were anxious to return to work, and with a regular air service, a storage compound and a crane available, I decided to lay up *Northabout* in Nome for the winter. Some winter preparation was needed: all ventilation openings were sealed to prevent driven snow entering, the exhaust was plugged, additional antifreeze was added to protect the engine to minus 50 degrees, the water tanks were drained and batteries, electrical equipment and tinned food were stored in our new-found friends' houses.

With *Northabout* secure we flew home via Anchorage and Seattle. As we were about to board the plane in Seattle on 11 September 2001 an air disaster in New York changed the world for the worse, forever.

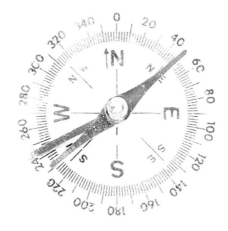

9

NORTHABOUT CRUISES
SOUTH FROM ALASKA

During the winter back home in Ireland, the next stage of the plan was worked out. Basically we would sail south and transit the Panama Canal, spend some time cruising the Caribbean, cross the Atlantic and sail home to Westport. This would give an opportunity to cruise down Alaska's and British Columbia's Inside Passage which has some of the most wonderful scenery and wildlife in the world. *Northabout* also was invited to appear at the metal boat festival in Vancouver, Washington State, which was on our route south.

The crew who had sailed the North West Passage had, in the main, used up all their holidays for some time to come but that was unlikely to be a major problem, as many of my friends had expressed an interest in sailing on *Northabout*. I was happy that Paddy Barry was available for the first leg starting from Nome and Michael Brogan would join us later for a couple of weeks. The rest of the crew were all new recruits but known to me. The distances to be travelled were great and changing crews involved a lot of planning. Finding suitable places with airports occupied quite some time. With a basic plan made, Paddy and I, plus our new recruits, flew to Nome to prepare for some easygoing cruising, or so we thought at the time. The crew for the first leg were Paddy

Top: Northabout at anchor in Lituya Bay.
Right: The Alaska crew – James Cahill,
Jarlath, Richard Browne, Micheline Egan
and John Magee.

and I, Michael McGarry, Richard Browne and Ben McDonagh.

Having wintered ashore in the harbour authority secure yard in Nome, we returned in early June 2002, and with minimal delay *Northabout* was launched and re-rigged. Worrying thoughts of problems like a frost-cracked engine or even the crane not being available were running through my mind. Despite the severe conditions endured during the winter, no major problems occurred, the engine cooling system being protected with antifreeze to withstand minus 40 degrees Celsius. It was a relief to be in the water again. We loaded the stores and re-installed the electronic equipment. At last we said goodbye to the ice and vowed never to sail in icy waters again!

Leaving our friends and the high living of Nome, we sailed towards False Pass in the Aleutian Islands, with stops at St Laurence and St Paul Islands. Once through False Pass in the Aleutian

Richard lowers the anchor at the Reid Glacier in Glacier Bay. We anchored for a time while we admired the wonderful scenery and wildlife.

Island chain, the change in climate was pronounced. Now, for the first time since leaving Ireland, we saw trees. Remarkably, some of them were thriving on rocky islets.

At Kodiak Island we were stormbound for over a week. An amusing sign ashore read, 'What to do in an emergency – if the sun shines', warranted no doubt by the rarity of sunshine there. Kodiak's harbour is home to a large fishing fleet and can accommodate 1,200 vessels of all sizes. All over Alaska the Russian influence is still visible, in the street names and in the buildings, particularly in the magnificent Russian Orthodox Church with its gold cupolas. This was a reminder of Alaskan history; America purchased Alaska from the Russians in 1867.

While we waited for the gales to pass, we enjoyed the nightly party in the pub. Every night we celebrated somebody's birthday. The attraction of Paddy's guitar playing and singing boosted the pub's turnover. Soon we were on first-name terms with everyone. In Kodiak we were introduced to an Alaskan custom – a bell suspended over the bar is rung when a skipper has had a good fishing trip, signalling that all the drinks are on him. No night passed without the bell tolling several times! On our last night, with the fishing boats all gone to sea, we found the bar staff and ourselves celebrating the dog's birthday! It was time to get out of there!

Top: *A playful sea Otter.* Right: *Jarlath had more luck at fishing than the 'fishermen' on board; one cast landed this 15lb salmon.*

After a thrash across the Gulf of Alaska in winds at times reaching force 8, we had a crew change at Seward. With our new crew, which included Micheline Egan, the first female crew member, we continued our trip south with stops at Yakutat and the magical Lituya Bay. We sought shelter in Lituya Bay from a gale and once inside its narrow entrance we sailed in calm waters to the glaciers at its head. The scenery was magnificent and the break from the heavy weather was a relief. In July 1958 this bay was devastated by a tsunami, generated by an earthquake, which resulted in the surrounding hills being submerged by seas. The high tide mark was recorded at a remarkable 1,720 feet above normal sea level.

In Yakutat we celebrated 4 July by joining the parade with our 'band'. The heavy weather continued until we reached Cape Spencer. With great relief we gained the shelter of the islands and entered the unbelievably calm waters of Cross Sound.

In Elfin Cove marina we got our first opportunity in a week to shower and wash our clothes. Micheline brought a civilising influence on board.

This unique, beautiful tiny village surrounds a bay. It claims to have the world's smallest highway – a narrow boardwalk on brackets fixed to the cliffs. This was the only access to the houses.

Northabout's route then followed the spectacular inside passage – the 'Marine Highway' as it is called in the guidebooks – whale watching, glacier viewing and enjoying the scenery. Paddy Barry had cynically remarked before he left us as planned in Seward, 'there is nothing in the inside passage except scenery'.

Clockwise from top: *Humpback whales breaching nearby; a collection of Indian carvings on Cormorant Island; trainee carvers are being taught the ancient craft and traditions from master craftsmen on Cormorant Island.*

We sailed into Glacier Bay having previously received a permit. Glacier Bay National Park and Preserve contains sixteen glaciers constantly creating multi-coloured icebergs. The ice has receded many miles inland from that shown on Captain Cook's chart in 1794 when the bay was completely filled with ice. The view of the Reid Glacier and the wildlife made the long detour worthwhile. We saw whales, sea otters, orcas and eagles in abundance. It was a pity about the intrusion of the many cruise ships that look so out of place there.

Prince Rupert was our entry port into Canada, where we were made very welcome. With crew now reduced to myself, Michael and Richard, we sailed with a fair wind down Johnstone Strait, Discovery Passage, and into Seymour Narrows with its fearsome tides.

Captain Vancouver, in his voyage of exploration in 1792, described the Seymour Narrows thus:

The tide, setting to the southwards through this confined passage, rushes with such immense impetuosity as to produce the appearance of falls considerably high; though not the least obstruction of either rocks or sand, as far as we had an opportunity of examining it, appeared to exist.

In fact, the mid channel was obstructed by an underwater rock known as Ripple Rock, which had less than three metres of water over it. This was removed by blasting in 1958 by the largest non-nuclear explosion ever recorded. To place the explosives it was necessary to construct a 1,000-metre long tunnel from the shore under the seabed, out to the rock. Earlier attempts to drill the rock from floating platforms failed disastrously, when the current swept everything away.

Our navigation needed detailed planning to work the tides; the GPS at times indicated speeds of over 12 knots.

One of the most interesting sites we visited was Alert Bay on Cormorant Island, where we visited the award-winning museum, the centre of Kwakiuti culture, which has a project teaching the younger generation the art of carving totem poles. Among the many other attractive sites were Telegraph Cove, Montague Harbour on Gabriola Island and the spectacular Louisa Inlet, with an extremely narrow entrance and a raging waterfall at its head. One could spend years enjoying the interesting cruising grounds around here.

A pleasant sail took us to Vancouver City, British Columbia. This was a complete contrast to our previous weeks in the wilderness. With its high-rise buildings, the city looks like Hong Kong from the sea, and indeed many of its new immigrants have come from that city.

In the maritime museum the *St Roch* is on display – Captain Larsen's vessel that sailed the North West Passage in 1942-43, returning in 1944.

✦✦✦

Sailing north to Prince Rupert. Left to right: Anne Doherty, Seamus Salmon, Rory Casey, Ben McDonagh, Mick Corrigan, Verina and Michelle Rowley.

We had wonderful sailing and anchorages in the Islands on route to Victoria. The city of Victoria has many attractions. In addition to all the street artists, musicians and entertainers there is much of maritime interest. The relatively inexpensive marina is right in the centre of the city and the harbour wall has bronze plaques honouring the achievements of various world-renowned sailors such as John Guzzwell, Susan and Eric Hiscock and Captain Voss. Incidentally *Tilikum*, the converted log canoe in which Voss sailed around the world, can be seen in the maritime museum. Guzzwell's *Trekka*, the 20 ft yacht in which he circumnavigated, is also on view in the nearby shopping mall.

Northabout had an invitation to the Metal Boat Festival in another Vancouver – in Washington State, USA, 260 miles away, including the 80 miles upstream on the mighty Columbia River.

On the way we called to Westport in Washington State, to give our regards from the Westport Town Council in Ireland. They were more interested in collecting dockage fees than in our felicitations.

We didn't stay long. A sign on the harbour wall, painted in big letters, read, 'Don't forget to tip your deck hand'.

Welcome to America!

The bar at the entrance to the Columbia River has a well-deserved fearsome reputation for breaking seas. In fact, the US Coastguard do their heavy weather training here. By timing the tides right we had no real difficulty in entering, and after a night in Ilwaco marina we continued upstream to Vancouver.

The Metal Boat Festival was a great success. We attended technical seminars on various marine topics and learned a lot from them. We made many new friends among people who thought and talked like us. *Northabout* was the festival's main attraction and I spent a long time showing its features to interested people. One bearded sailor remarked, 'A great boat, well built and ready for sea but the paint job sucks!' – *Northabout's* finish is unpainted aluminium.

Time had run out and our sailing season was over. With the help of a contact made at the festival, we were introduced to a quiet private marina at an affordable rate in another Westport, in a small creek off the Columbia River near Astoria. This Westport was in Oregon.

Northabout was laid up afloat for the winter under the watchful eye of Chuck, a live-aboard who was completing the interior fit out of his steel boat nearby.

Maybe because of the heat (over 100 degrees) endured in Oregon, the attraction of the Panama Canal route home diminished and finally vanished. During the winter back home in Ireland, a new plan emerged.

Why not complete the circle and sail home via the North East Passage?

Why not indeed?

During the next summer of 2003, with a variety of crew members, *Northabout* retraced its route north to Prince Rupert, where it was laid up, prepared and provisioned for its greatest test yet.

Before leaving Westport, Oregon, Tom Moran, Brendan Minish and I spent a week working on *Northabout*. Tom removed the overworked gearbox, completely stripped it down and replaced all the oil seals and gaskets. Brendan overhauled all the electronics and reinstalled the overhauled autopilot. Now everything worked properly again for the next challenge, thanks to the two technical 'wizards'.

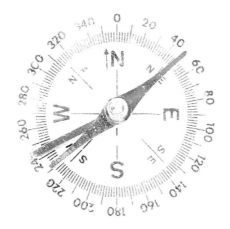

10

PRINCE RUPERT
TO ANADYR

Liquid sunshine – that's how the locals humorously describe the rain that falls incessantly in Prince Rupert, British Colombia, Canada. Well, it makes a pleasant change from the 104-degree temperature of Oregon. Never again, we said, as we left the ice astern in 2001. Never again will we probe our way through ice fields with hands numbed from pushing ice floes aside with ice poles. But inexplicably, here we were again getting ready for our greatest challenge yet, our attempt to traverse the North East Passage. The North East Passage, or as the Russians know it, the Northern Sea Route, extends from the Bering Straits and continues westward north of the Russian mainland through the frozen waters of Siberia towards Norway's North Cape.

I selected Prince Rupert (known locally as Rupert) as a good point of departure for fitting out for an Arctic expedition, conveniently located at the Canadian/Alaskan border. It is the second largest town in British Colombia, with a population of 26,000. Set in a spectacular location surrounded by mountains, it has a deep-water port, a marina and an airport. Helpful customs officials pointed out that as we were creating employment by having work done on board while in Rupert we would be exempt from taxes. This was in sharp contrast to our experience in Nome,

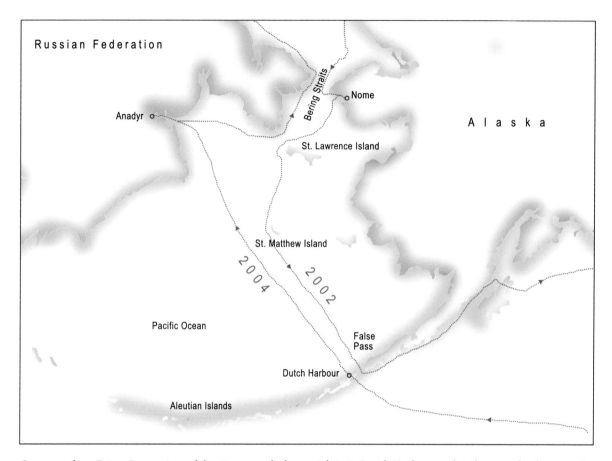

Our route from Prince Rupert (out of the picture on the lower right) via Dutch Harbour in the Aleutian Islands to Anadyr in Russia.

Alaska, where in addition to all the other storage bills we were presented with a bill for 'City Taxes' of $630.

Northabout was laid up afloat for the winter at Rushbrook Marina. A bald eagle had taken up residence on the masthead, depositing a layer of droppings on deck. A two-inch thick growth of mussels and slime grew below the waterline. Apart from that, all was well on board; all that it needed was a good scrub. After spending a futile two days trying to get a crane or travel-lift to haul out for a bottom scrub, we were offered the use of the nearby Prince Rupert Yacht Club's drying grid.

Between the huge tides we dried out and with the club's power washer we blasted off the marine growth and eagle droppings. Soon all was spick and span again, with new anti-fouling applied, sails hoisted and furled and engine serviced.

Nearly all supplies and services are available in Rupert as it is a major fishing port. The only notable missing service is a travel lift capable of lifting out a vessel as big as *Northabout*.

We had shipped three crates of supplies to Rupert containing our polar clothing, some rations, musical instruments, engine spare parts and equipment. All the supplies were loaded on board,

Top: *Ready for a bottom scrub.*
Left: *Tom and Joan playing a tune in Prince Rupert.*

including a vast supply of food and drink purchased locally. We were provisioning for two seasons in the ice; the availability of supplies in Siberia was uncertain.

The crew for the first leg to Anadyr were Paddy Barry and I, Tom Moran, Joan Bourke, Brendan Minish and Eoin McAllister. Tom was a great addition to the crew, with his knowledge of engines, his cooking and mandolin playing. Tom was familiar with *Northabout*, having rebuilt the gearbox the previous year in Westport, Oregon. Joan, in addition to being a sailor, was a first-class fiddle

Dutch Harbour in the Aleutian Islands. Looking down at the harbour entrance in the background, the buildings visible are fish-processing factories.

player; Brendan, our radio man, was taking a break from his role as base man and soon had all our electronic equipment de-bugged. Eoin was a sailor and singer. Our night-time headquarters was set up in Solly's bar on the outskirts of town, where we played music and were entertained. We were soon on first-name terms with many of the fine people of Rupert.

Brendan installed our latest electronic toy, a laptop computer with digitised charts on the hard drive, which when linked to the GPS showed our position on the screen, and much more.

Not having full confidence in electronic technology, we also carried paper charts as back up, and I'm happy to say the electronic charts worked flawlessly. A monitor wind vane self-steering system was also installed. This was a great help in the long Pacific crossing, where it steered for days on end without complaint. The electrically-operated autopilot was also installed, having been completely rebuilt; it too performed flawlessly, not wanting to be outdone by the monitor. As we waited for a series of depressions to pass we completed most of the maintenance work that a boat demands, and on 7 July 2004 we departed from Prince Rupert, destined for Dutch Harbour in the Aleutian Islands on the first leg of the Pacific crossing to Anadyr, Russia.

I have to go back a little to describe the North East Passage and the process of getting the permit to sail in Russian waters firstly though.

The North East Passage is different from the North West Passage in several ways:

- ✦ The distance is 50 per cent greater overall.
- ✦ The lands bordering the passage are generally barren and devoid of interest.
- ✦ The prevailing currents flow eastward – against us.
- ✦ The languages spoken are those of the northern nomads and Russian – we are not fluent in either.
- ✦ The permit to transit the Northern Sea Route is difficult to obtain.

Paddy had spent all his spare time during the previous winter applying for the permits and seeking information on the transit of the Northern Sea Route. He spoke with Arved Fuchs and Eric Brossier, both of whom had recently sailed the Northern Sea Route. While the stated aim of the northern sea route administration is to encourage shipping to use the route, it seemed that every obstacle was being put in our way. Firstly we must have a Russian 'partner' through whom all correspondence must be routed. We must also have on board an ice pilot, supplied by the Murmansk Shipping Company. We were lucky that Michael Brogan's brother Colm was a businessman living in Moscow,

Tom, Joan and Brendan practice ropework.

The earlier influence of Russia in Alaska makes its presence felt here with the Russian Orthodox Church at the entrance to Dutch Harbour.

a fluent Russian speaker, who understood how business is done in Russia. Colm agreed to join us for the voyage, and without his knowledge of the system we would still be waiting for the permit. Paddy had earlier travelled to Moscow with Colm and met with the officials of the Department of Economic Development and Trade. A partner was found, terms agreed, applications made, visas applied for and then we waited for answers.

Up to the time of our leaving Ireland, the permit had not been received. We therefore arranged that Colm would collect the permit in Moscow and bring it with him to Anadyr. Paddy and I had not received our Russian visas either; we arranged that they be couriered to Dutch Harbour. This meant we had to have another copy of our passports to enter US territory at Dutch Harbour. To enter US territory on a private yacht it is necessary to have a US visa – the usual visa waiver is not accepted. As it happened we entered USA on passport number one, and collected passport number 2 with Russian visa, in Dutch Harbour. As one can imagine, this was all very worrying and stressful and was prone to Murphy's law: if anything can go wrong, it will happen at the most inconvenient moment. This time we were lucky nothing went wrong.

The 1,320 mile crossing to Dutch Harbour was uneventful; good sailing most of the way. In crossing the Gulf of Alaska the direct route took us across seamounts – underwater mountains 400 metres below the surface. We quickly learned to avoid these as they create rough seas.

As we approached Unalaska Island and Unimak Pass, we had a strong blow from ahead and an adverse tide. The pilot book warns of rip tides, whirlpools and williwaws. With the engine on full revs, we could only make 3 knots headway but once in the shelter of the land our speed improved and by midnight we tied up at the small boat harbour, in Dutch Harbour.

As we entered the port the copper dome of the Russian Orthodox Church stood out as a reminder of the Russian influence here in earlier times. Snow lay in the gullies and on the higher mountains. The town's economy is based on fishing; all around the port were the fish-processing factories and the fishing boats on which this port thrives. This is the most productive US fishing port, both in tonnage and in value. Most people in town are involved in the fishing industry directly or indirectly.

The fish-processing workers are mainly Filipino, Russian, Vietnamese and Mexican contract workers who live in the company hostels. The fishing vessels are huge, from 70-foot trawlers and crabbers to 600-foot factory ships that fish these lucrative waters, living on the edge of fear during the fishing season, which coincides with the winter months. The profits can be huge; a fine deck hand's share of the season's catch can in a season pay for a new house. But the risks are enormous; many lives are lost working on ice-covered decks in gale force winds.

Few of the original native people remain. The history of their enslavement makes sad reading. They were initially exploited by the Russian fur traders and then by their American successors. The final ignominy came during the Second World War when the Americans, fearing that the native Aleuts might be sympathetic to the Japanese, rounded them up and held them in concentration camps for most of the war. The Japanese bombed Dutch Harbour in 1942 and occupied the westernmost Aleutian islands of Attu and Kiska for a time before being routed later with great loss of life on both sides.

Left: *Giant crab pots for catching King Crabs.* Right: *The Elbow Room, the most famous pub in Alaska. In former times it had a reputation for rowdiness.*

Chris Gannon, a native of Westport now living in Dutch Harbour, greeted us in the morning, attracted by our tricolour. Chris took us around town shopping while he caught up with the latest news from home. Most importantly we collected our passports which were delivered by Federal Express. With visas to enter Russia secure in our hands, we were able to relax in the 'Elbow Room', a famous pub, well known to Alaskan fishermen. This pub had the reputation in the old days of being the second most rowdy pub in the USA. I never found out the name of the number one contender!

Noting the lack of females around the island, Pat told us there was a woman hiding behind every tree. The irony, of course, is that there are no trees! After a few days sightseeing and mountain climbing, we visited the museums and other sights. Once we had re-fuelled and re-stocked with food, we departed on Tuesday 16 July bound for Anadyr, 800 miles away.

On Thursday morning we passed south of the Priblof islands clearly visible about 10 miles away. All were working well on board; in addition to standing their regular watches, Tom, Eoin, and Joan produced excellent meals. Brendan had our e-mail system working and made regular radio contacts with amateur radio enthusiasts all over the world.

The latest e-mail received from the Irish embassy created a flurry of activity.

Paddy continues:

We had been at sea for a day and a half, the contrary wind had eased and we were settling into the passage. An e-mail from the Irish Embassy arrived via radio link, with the devastating message:

The Federal Border Guard Service has informed the Irish Embassy in Moscow that it had NOT given clearance for the voyage of Northabout *and that, until such time as such clearance was issued, the boat and its crew WOULD NOT BE WELCOME.*

The options were to alter course for Nome, Alaska, to heave to at sea until the permit could be sorted, or to go back to Dutch Harbour.

We chose the fourth option – to keep going, and sort out the problem on the satellite phone.

Calls were made to the Irish Embassy in Moscow, to Colm and our partner Alexei in Moscow, and Kevin in Dublin.

Since our visit to Moscow last December to lodge our permit application, all 60 pages of it translated into Russian, we had known that this was no foregone conclusion. But Colm had been to Moscow twice since, been to the heart of the system, with our partner Alexei Zdanov, and we thought we had the permit sorted.

And so it was but we didn't know it until a couple of days later, when we were about 40 miles westward of Glory of Russia Cape on Saint Matthew Island.

Now with light hearts we carried on, crossed the international dateline and sat round the cabin table to a 'dateline dinner' – and a very fine and relaxed meal it was. The wind now filled the sails from the starboard quarter. What a relief to be able to cut the engine! Our wind-vane steered the boat as we joked, yarned and then brought out the music, with Joan on the fiddle, Tom on the mandolin, and mé féin on the guitar. And surprise surprise, Jarlath on harmonica – what a dark horse. I think we exceeded our 1-beer-per-man-per-day quota that night.

Our watches passed easily, three hours on, in pairs, six hours off: no hardship about that. The nights grew brighter so on the day before we reached Anadyr I rigged a 'curtain' over the portholes in my cabin, for darkness – Arctic nights again. About 100 miles out, the weather closed in, fog all around. The sea water grew brown. We were seeing the effect of the Anadyr river, 700 miles long, discharging its muddy water.

With GPS, radar and depth-sounder, we were aware that we were within 5 miles of Anadyr and still had seen nothing, not a ship, nor shore. We heard voices on the VHF radio, in Russian, naturally enough. The big test came – with my call to Anadyr Radio – all my efforts at learning Russian were now about to be put to the test. And it seemed to work; they acknowledged our call and asked that we change to Channel 15. There we heard nothing!

Anyway, it didn't matter. We were now in the estuary, and could see where we were going; very industrial indeed, with the tower blocks of this 10,000 population capital of Chukotka on the hill behind. The berth we took, the only one we could see, was open to the wind and waves. Getting lines ashore and tied required some acrobatics.

With difficulty we got Northabout *secured to the battered pier, only to be told to move again as we were tied up at the ferry berth. We moved around the corner to a more sheltered berth, in the driving rain.*

Then it began – the men in uniform arrived. How I wished Colm, our Russian speaker, was here. My best wishes and greetings from Ireland didn't seem to cut much ice with these men. I was taken in a van through the town to a gate where the armed sentry saluted and waved us through. Tales from Solzhenitsyn passed through my mind. The room to which I was taken had 'Major' printed on the door– at least that's what I think it said. He couldn't have been more helpful over the next couple of hours as he explained that Chukotka was a 'closed' area and that we shouldn't be here – the communication from Moscow had not been so good. I explained, as best I could, that the rest of our crew would be arriving in from Moscow that evening with our permit, our Russian speaker and with our State Ice Pilot. I think the major phoned Moscow, regardless of the nine-hour time difference, and I was given document. Formalities were completed. Great smiles all round. On the way back to the boat we stopped at a bank so I could change dollars to roubles.

In the meantime, back on the boat, curious visitors were starting to call. They don't get too many sailing boats here – none at all, in fact. One man had come from the airport and was able to tell us that our Irish friends had arrived. Their story of baggage retrieval would fill a page.

And to bring our story right up to date, here we are in Anadyr, all together after a great night in the Chukotka Hotel, sore heads to prove it. Tom, Joan, Brendan and Eoin are packing their bags and tomorrow are flying back to Moscow and Ireland.

Rory Casey, Mike Brogan, Kevin Cronin, Garry Finnegan, Colm Brogan and Vladimir Samolovich are moving their gear on board. The town is a building site, a lot of Turkish building workers among the Russians and indigenous Chukchi. They all seem friendly.

We're taking on diesel and water. Tomorrow we hope to be on our way.

A few words from Kevin one of the arriving team members.

We flew from the new Moscow airport but just when we thought all was in-hand, our flight was delayed for seven hours. The arrival in Anadyr was memorable, three hours waiting for our passports (even though everything was in order), a scrum for baggage reclaim, and then a helter-skelter mini-bus ride on a mudtrack. This was followed by a short ferry ride across the Anadyr river, and even though it was raining, we spotted at least a dozen whales (belugas) and lots of seals. It was great to see Northabout *tied up at the pier.*

Jarlath continues.

As we waited for Paddy to deal with immigration, the port captain, a very affable man, produced a document in Russian for my signature. In case I couldn't understand the Russian version he gave me a copy in English for my information. I readily agreed to all the conditions!

Sunken vessels in the port of Anadyr.

94

OBLIGATORY INSTRUCTION
CAPTAIN ON FOREIGN SHIP ON ORGANISZATION
AND CARRYING SERVICES IN ANADYR SEAPORT

1. Service on board ship must be organized by change sailors.
2. To ensure an admission mode on ship, keep count strangers of persons visiting ship. Visitors to miss on the ship only on gaps of immigration service, Dockers – on gaps of immigration service at crew list presence.
3. To delay all persons, forting penetrate on the ship or come off it without install documents and send their ordinary immigration service.
4. Attentively check the documents beside persons visiting ship, fix a time VWV call at; drop in on the ship and slope. The documents of visitors of ship to keep before the slope of these persons in the install place, ensuring their safety and proper checking.
5. To know, who from crew members of ship not rarefied slope on the coast and stop attempts in the install place, ensuring their safety and proper checking.
6. Constantly know an amount of crew members inhering ashore, but in the same way workers and other persons, missed on the ship, and check their return.
7. Not to alllow VWV wear out from ships on the coast or from the coast on the ship of weapon, ammunitions and the others, forbidden to import in RF or export from RF subjects and material. In the event of revealing such attempts frontier service (call 2-06-58)
8. When arising the sharp situations (disturbances, provacative and other illlegitimate actions) immediately frontier service,
9. To fulfill requirements employees of frontier service, checking service sailor.
10. Seasonally examine adjoining to the external board of ship water surface. In the course of bunkering a ship or other operations to lead an observation fir the service ship, being near its board.

SAILOR IS FORBIDDEN:

1. To abandon a place of carrying a service before change.
2. To miss anyone from ships or on the ship outside of the install order.
3. To use alcohol drink at a period of carrying service.

Distracted from the service by other actions, not provided official instructions.

Frontier authorities of Anadyr Seaport hope,
that captain of ship with the whole responsibility to given rules.
Upon default of given requirements a captain of ship
will have responsibility on Russian laws.

In the Port of Anadyr; Slava, our Russian ice-pilot, with Joan and the helpful port captain, trying to communicate.

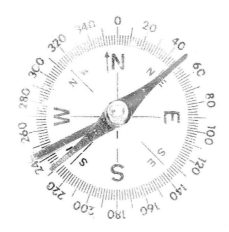

11

COMMUNICATIONS

(OF PARTICULAR INTEREST TO RADIO ENTHUSIASTS!)

BRENDAN MINISH

In the spring of 2001 Jarlath Cunnane got in touch with me regarding the possibility of acting as the base radio operator for the forthcoming Irish North West Passage trip that was due to depart in June 2001.

Initially the focus was on the possibility of making voice contacts once or twice a week as had been done on previous voyages.

As it turned out, the timing was good. I had already been experimenting with some of the new digital communications systems for use on HF (High-Frequency). One system in particular seemed especially relevant to the forthcoming trip. This was a combination of Pactor 2 (a robust, error-correcting mode of transmission able to transfer digital data efficiently and reliably over HF radio), Winlink 2000 – WL2K (a system for handling email over radio using Pactor that is free for use by licensed amateur radio operators. It works well under radio conditions that are too poor to support voice contact) and Airmail (the client software used on board to connect to the WL2K system via radio using Pactor). One of the features of Airmail is that it will also allow back-to-back connections

Brendan in his radio shack in Castlebar, Ireland, forwarding an ice chart to Northabout.

between Airmail users. This allowed traffic to be sent directly from Ireland to *Northabout* when radio conditions permitted.

Airmail is written and supported by Jim Corenman, KE6RK. Jim is a cruising sailor who uses Pactor as his primary means of staying in touch with friends and family. Jim very kindly provided me with the server version of Airmail which made it easy for me to route *Northabout's* e-mail to and from the Internet.

One of the issues facing radio communication with the Arctic is that auroral activity is very common, sometimes lasting for days. One of the effects of auroral activity is that it often degrades radio communications and sometimes causes complete radio blackouts.

When radio conditions were not good enough to permit direct connections traffic could also be handled via the Winlink system. There were a number of North American WL2K stations that would be used during the voyage to pass traffic but one station in particular had consistently good signals to the northern Canadian Arctic. This Station is VE1YZ located in Halifax Nova Scotia and operated by Neil Hughes. Neil took a personal interest in the voyage and was tremendously helpful with ensuring that the WL2K system carried relevant weather and ice information for the various polar regions that *Northabout* has travelled through.

My involvement with the project began whilst *Northabout* was still under construction. This provided an excellent opportunity to ensure that the design of the HF antenna system was suitable for long-distance communications with Ireland. Marine HF antenna systems are always a compromise and *Northabout's* antenna system is no exception to this rule.

Northabout's antenna system consists of a section of the backstay tuned by an automatic antenna tuner. This length was chosen to provide good long-distance communications off the stern of the boat. The primary compromise here was reduced performance in the direction of the bow of the boat, not an issue for the North West Passage trip and no one had even mentioned the North East Passage at that stage.

We had to install an antenna mast and large directional antenna system at my end to improve our chances of maintaining regular contact. This in itself was quite a feat of civil engineering that I could not have completed without the able assistance of Jarlath and Padraic Baynes, whose radio call was EI9JA, as well as plenty of help from the members of the MREN, our local, amateur radio club.

The radio chosen for *Northabout* was the Icom IC 728. This is an early 1990's model, which allowed for a spare radio to be carried on board.

We also had time to test all the radio equipment destined for installation on *Northabout* to ensure that it would perform as expected once installed on board. There were a few surprises here but these were resolved in time for the launch.

When *Northabout* was launched we installed and tested her radio systems. This also provided Gearóid O'Riain with a chance to learn about the radio and IT system that he was to manage on board. Luckily Gearóid learned fast in the week before the departure of *Northabout*.

Once *Northabout* was underway we established a routine consisting of a daily radio schedule with more frequent schedules being run on days where there were additional needs for up-to-date information. During these schedules we would exchange *Northabout's* e-mail and I would pass on up-to-date weather and ice information. I would also get an updated position report. After these exchanges had taken place we would occasionally transfer digital photographs and other updates for the website.

Initially we also had a schedule of voice contacts but maintaining voice contact proved to be much harder than maintaining our Pactor schedules. Voice communications require much better radio conditions than Pactor and radio conditions were often poor or very poor due to the regular auroral activity.

On occasions where radio conditions were too poor for direct communications with Ireland, *Northabout* was usually successful in making contact with the WL2K system via VE1YZ. Overall this system worked very well and there were only a few days when *Northabout* was unable to make any contact.

On the voyage between Gjoahaven and Cambridge Bay a fault occurred with the automatic antenna tuner. This also caused the failure of the HF radio. Thankfully Jarlath and Gearóid were

Brendan's rotating directional antenna in his garden. As we moved position, he rotated his antenna to get the best radio signal to Northabout.

able to repair the tuner. The radio, however, required more extensive repairs so the spare HF radio was pressed into service for the remainder of the voyage.

Equipment on board for the HF communications system in 2001:

HF radio Icom IC 728
Spare HF radio Icom IC728
Pactor modem SCS PTC2e
Antenna tuning unit SGC SG-230 smartuner automatic antenna tuning unit
Laptop computer

Web links:
Winlink – www.winlink.org
Airmail – www.airmail2000.com
Icom – www.icomuk.co.uk
SCS – www.scs-ptc.com
SGC – www.sgcworld.com

In 2003 Tom Moran and I accompanied Jarlath to Westport, Oregon, to assist with repairs and bring the boat northwards to Seattle, Washington State.

The boat's electrical systems and radio equipment had held out well, so relatively little work was needed in this area. To test all the systems we sailed to Seattle. The voyage was uneventful and enjoyable. We were able to stay in touch with home via the Winlink system which has excellent coverage in this region.

For me, one of the pleasures of sailing aboard *Northabout* has been keeping in touch with friends in the amateur radio community using *Northabout's* radio system. My favourite mode of communications for this is also one of the oldest – Morse code. Morse code has many advantages: it's efficient at getting through even with weak signals and, due to the near universal use of a standard set of abbreviations, it is effective in crossing language barriers. Morse code is also relatively unobtrusive to the other members of the crew if headphones are worn.

The North East Passage Trip

The North East Passage trip communications needs presented a similar set of challenges to the North West Passage trip and we already had most of the groundwork done. There were, however, a few differences that had to be taken into account.

Northabout would be travelling in a much more remote part of the world and there would be little chance of accessing the WL2K system on anything more than an occasional basis. This meant that the communications would rely heavily on making regular radio contact with Ireland.

Northabout would be relying on electronic charts. This meant that there would be a need to have two computers on board in good working order. This actually provided a useful means of having some redundant equipment on board. The computer for charting was capable of being used for communications and the communications computer also had the electronic charting software installed on it. Computer equipment can, however, generate radio interference; this is the last thing you need if you are relying on using weak signals that have travelled many thousands of miles from Ireland.

It was a requirement of the Russian authorities that *Northabout* carry a hand-held satellite phone and that daily satellite phone contact be maintained with Murmansk. An iridium portable satellite phone was acquired.

It was felt that it would be beneficial, in case of emergency, to have a portable HF radio that could be used to summon assistance should the need to abandon the boat in the ice occur. For this purpose an ex-military HF man pack radio was sourced and a battery-charging regime devised to keep it in a condition ready for use.

Pactor as a transmission system had been improved. Speed and reliability had both been improved. Pactor 3 offered us a very useful performance increase and only required software upgrades to our Pactor controllers.

Rory Casey was replacing Gearóid O'Riain as the on board communications/IT specialist for the North East Passage voyage. Rory would have to learn how it all worked whilst in Ireland and he did an admirable job.

Jarlath had studied for and obtained his amateur radio licence. Not only did *Northabout* now have two licence holders on board but Jarlath had also learned how to operate and troubleshoot the radio equipment.

In 2004 I joined *Northabout* in Prince Rupert, British Colombia, to assist with the preparations for the North East Passage trip and to take part in the delivery voyage to Anadyr in Russia. This provided the opportunity to ensure that all radio and communications equipment was working correctly. We replaced *Northabout's* marine VHF and antenna; the antenna had been damaged by water ingress and the VHF was showing its age, as well as having been repaired on a number of occasions. This left *Northabout* with a spare working VHF and reliable working primary VHF.

For the delivery trip from Prince Rupert to Anadyr we relied extensively on the WK2K system but once we got within a couple of days of Anadyr we were very much on the edge of reliable WL2K communications. After Anadyr we would not be able to establish HF radio communications until I was able to get back to Ireland.

Initially radio communications between Ireland and *Northabout* were difficult but as *Northabout* made westerly progress and shortened the distance communications, conditions improved, even allowing voice contacts, some of which coincided with prominent GAA football games!

In 2005, after spending the winter in Khatanga, all the radio and communications equipment was found to be in good working order, although there were some issues with the grounding system due to corrosion. Rory and Jarlath diagnosed and repaired the grounding connections. Making a long-lasting and sound connection between aluminium and copper is not an easy task in a marine environment.

There was one other issue that caused us some concern with communications in 2005. *Northabout* had a new interference problem that was hampering her ability to receive signals from Ireland. This made communications more difficult on occasion and was eventually diagnosed in Norway as the

power supply for a new laptop that was being used for the electronic charts. All the equipment had been given a clean bill of health from an interference perspective in 2004 but the new laptop came with a new power supply that generated considerable interference.

12

SOCIAL PATTERNS
AND WILDLIFE

MICHAEL BROGAN

In the native languages of many of the different peoples who inhabit the Arctic, the word for 'hunter' is the same is the same as the word for 'man'. A good hunter is highly respected within his community, because it is through his skills the people can exist in the harsh environment of the far north. Knowledge of the environment and climate, gained over years, and handed down from generation to generation, has enabled the people to survive both spiritually and physically. 'To know the land is to prosper.'

The inhabitants across the far north have one thing in common – their ability to survive in a wilderness hostile to human habitation, mostly iced over, and darkened by a long polar night. This need to survive has led to a close relationship between the animals, the people, and the climate. The hunting of animals in order to eat has been the basis of the way of life for the Arctic people ever since they arrived, as a result of the great human migrations from central Asia between the tenth and thirteenth centuries. Until the seventeenth century the Arctic people had no contact with any

A happy couple in Enuremo.

European civilisation, and called themselves 'Uit', 'Yupic', 'Inuit', etc, all meaning, the real people.

People all across the Arctic believe that animals, like humans, have souls, and must be respected, and that hunted animals chose to give themselves up for the benefit of the people, who in return must treat them with respect and dignity. They believe that the human body, like the bodies of animals, is no more than a covering of flesh that houses an 'energy', a 'life force', a 'spirit soul'. Rites and rituals still have a place in the everyday lives of the people. For instance, when hunting, Chuckchis constantly murmur magical spells in the belief that the hunted animal spirits can hear them, and their wives at home also utter spells, designed to urge the animals towards the hunters. Many taboos affect the behaviour of hunters. A good hunter speaks modestly, and it is forbidden for him to speak the word that describes the animal he is hunting.

Every animal that is killed as a result of hunting is the object of ritual ceremonies, which are

Top: *Our first sightings of walrus.* Above: *Working dogs on the street in Enuremo.*

designed to preserve and respect it, and return it to its 'spirit soul'. If the ritual is carried out properly, it is the belief that future hunts for that animal will be successful.

Many coastal communities lived in total isolation until relatively recently by hunting and fishing. In their diet, the meat and fat of the marine animals occupies a dominant position, and nothing of the animal goes to waste. As well as providing food, the animal also provides essential clothing, bedding, floor carpeting and roofing for the home. The blubber provides lighting and heat, and the skin is used for their drums, kayaks and umiaks. Handcrafted carvings and tools are fashioned from walrus and narwhal tusks, the ribs and jawbones of the whale, and the antlers of the caribou. In order not to offend the animal, all its parts must be used beneficially. Clothing made from the animal's skin must be beautiful and kept in good repair.

Although the native people may be living nowadays in relatively modern, and mostly small urban communities, their ties to the land are still very strong, in spite of the negative impact European domination has had on their culture. Their knowledge and use of the animals in their environment is the key to maintaining their traditional ways, and the survival of their communities.

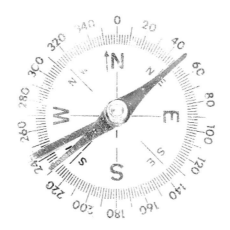

13

ANADYR TO TIKSI

Anadyr was in the middle of a building boom: new road surfaces, new pavements, new buildings and the refurbishment of old apartment blocks. Surprisingly the workers were mainly foreign: Canadians with their skill in timber-framed housing, Turkish road builders, and workers from the Russian republics. The apartments looked great in their new colours – we didn't realise then that this was the last time we would see a flash of colour in a Russian town. Apartments throughout Russia come in two standard sizes – 'fivers' and 'niners' – five storeys high or nine, all in the same drab grey colour.

On our first night ashore we enjoyed a Russian meal in the best hotel in town. Afterwards this developed into a traditional Irish music session with the combined band of the incoming and outgoing crew. The line-up was – Michael Brogan and Joan Bourke on fiddles, Tom Moran on mandolin, on guitars Paddy, Rory and Gary, with Kevin on bodhrán, Eoin on vocals and Jarlath on harmonica. The music was wonderful, or so we thought! Slava was bewildered at first but soon entered the party spirit and gave a splendid performance of Cossack dancing. An Australian television crew captured the scene on camera, which was later broadcast in Australia; we are still getting enquiries about doing an Australian tour.

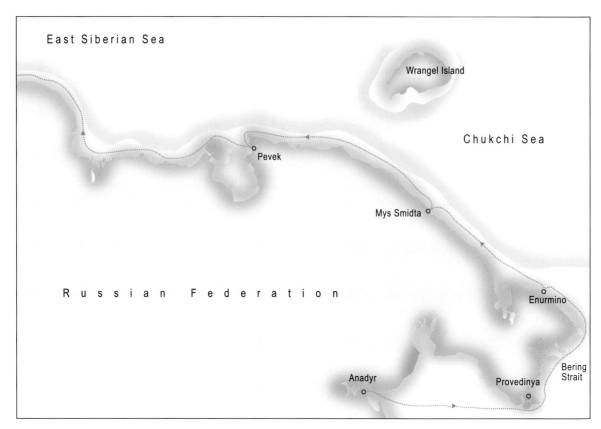

Above: *Map from Anadyr to Pevek, showing our stops at Enurimo and Mys Schmidt.*
Right: *The delivery crew in Anadyr after their Pacific crossing. Left to right: Joan Bourke, Eoin McAllister, Tom Moran, Brendan Minish, Jarlath Cunnane and Paddy Barry.*

In the morning it was back to reality though. Tom, Brendan, Eoin and Joan departed on the plane to Moscow and the new crew moved aboard.

The new crew joining Paddy and I were – Kevin Cronin, Rory Casey, Colm Brogan, Michael Brogan, Gary Finnegan and our Russian ice pilot, Slava. We had all sailed together in the past, with the exception of Slava and Gary. Gary was making a film for television and I liked the 'cut of his

Michael alighting from the Anadyr airport bus. There is a shortage of vehicle washing facilities in Russia!

jib'. Since he was a good mixer and a musician, I knew he would fit in well with us. I was a little more apprehensive about Slava. Though he had sailed on large ships all his life, this was his first time on board a small yacht, where he wouldn't have the same facilities and also, his knowledge of English was basic.

Considering all, he settled in fairly well, though it was difficult at times keeping him informed and feeling that he was part of our team. He, of course, was in a similarly difficult position with us – seven Irishmen with a common bond, as he was the only Russian.

Before we could depart we had to re-fuel and fill our water tanks. And most importantly, *Northabout* had to be surveyed by Slava before we could complete departure formalities. Slava took his responsibility seriously – he studied the construction plans and went through all the safety features thoroughly before declaring himself satisfied. Eventually he gave us the all clear. He assisted in negotiating the purchase of a fill of diesel from a vessel in the port. The water supply was more elusive. As there are no taps on the pier in Anadyr, water is delivered by tanker. The water tanker failed to show up as promised but after many phone calls water was eventually delivered later. Interestingly the water cost almost as much as the diesel. All this took time; everybody was helpful, especially the port captain, but formalities are tedious in Russia and nothing can be rushed.

Eventually we were free to leave and on Wednesday 28 July at 16.00 we departed in a light southerly wind, bound for Pevek, 975 miles away.

The Australian film crew were flying to a whaling festival in St Laurence Bay. As this was on our way, we decided to join in the festivities. Captain Cook named this bay when he anchored there

We negotiated a good cash deal for the supply of diesel from this vessel in Anadyr port.

on St Laurence's feast day during his voyage of discovery. This was also Captain Bob Bartlett's destination, having sledged from west of Cape Vankaren to seek help for his shipwrecked crew, from the ill-fated *Karluk,* marooned on Wrangel Island.

The weather was beautiful; brilliant sunshine and warm. All crew were in T-shirts as we sailed along the coast.

As we approached St Laurence Bay we noted that the hills in the background bristled with antennae, presumably a legacy from the Cold War. The town had an industrial appearance and looked like it had seen better days. As we approached, a plane took off and buzzed us several times. On the VHF radio, Slava was in communication with an agitated person ashore who was demanding permits. On hearing the word 'permit' we quickly decided that the whaling festival was not a priority at the moment and, hoisting sail, plotted a course towards Cape Dezhnev. In continuing good weather, we crossed the International Date-line again, going back from the 29 to 28 July.

Cape Dezhnev, with its lighthouse and memorial to Semen Dezhnev in the Bering Straits, was left astern on Saturday 31 July. Dezhnev's voyage is almost forgotten today, yet it ranks with the great voyages of Columbus and Magellen. Dezhnev, who sailed from the Kolma river in 1648 with 90 men in seven boats, was the first European to sail through the straits which are now called the Bering Straits, to the Anadyr river.

Clockwise from top: *Approaching Cape Dezhnev, the most easterly point of Asia, with Rory at the bow; a young woman in Enuremo; a street in Enuremo.*

Having rounded Cape Dezhnev, the most easterly point of Asia, and the prominent Cape Eulen, we later anchored off the mile-long sandy beach of Enurimo. Ashore we met the indigenous Chukchis who exist by hunting and whaling. They are permitted to take three whales, 30 walrus and an unlimited amount of seals annually. Their housing was basic timber shacks in poor condition, though a couple of new, good quality houses have been built recently.

We went ashore by dinghy and met the mayor and the local people, who were most welcoming, though I'm sorry to say some were the worse for wear from vodka. The children were delighted with our gifts of chocolate bars, and went off to get their mothers, who also had a craving for chocolate. One man pursued us, relentlessly trying to communicate in his native language. Eventually we learned what he was trying to say – he wanted video tape for his camcorder. Happily, Gary was able to supply him with it. Similarly another man tried to sell us gemstones, which we declined, not knowing their value.

Amundsen was forced to spend a winter here in 1920-21 when the *Maud,* on its North East Passage journey, became trapped in the ice. The mayor was aware of the story of his overwintering.

We got underway after three hours and made good progress. The weather was now much colder, as one would expect at this latitude. The thermal underwear, mid layer and waterproof outer layer was the norm now. A variety of hats were worn, some crewmen even wore two (on a two-hat day). Dubarry leather boots were good for most conditions, particularly when worn with thermal socks. Various gloves and mittens were worn; there seemed to be no consensus on the best solution – none was entirely satisfactory.

Soon we saw the ominous sign of ice ahead; ice blink, a reflection of the sea ice in the sky. To encounter ice so soon into the voyage was disappointing; we had hoped to have ice-free conditions for much longer. Our proposed diversion to Wrangel Island was not now possible. Sea ice firmly

Jarlath and new friends in Enuremo, with Northabout *at anchor off the beach.*

Walrus on the ice; we smelt them before we saw them!

blocked our route to the Island. Soon the ice was visible and its chilling effect was felt too. As we approached the ice, we saw a large pod of walrus on the ice. We were able to get quite close to them without them showing any sign of fear. We were all amazed at the sheer size of these creatures; Rory claimed they were bigger than cows.

The ice was impenetrable at that point, so we diverted towards the shore, looking for a shore lead. Hugging the shore we found a lead where the ice was lighter –about 1/10 ice, navigable with care. For hours we pushed and probed and crashed into sea ice, diverting around the heavier floes, as we forced our way westwards.

Once we saw ice, Slava became a different man; this was his territory, his specialised field of knowledge. He took over, pointing out leads, instructing us to turn to port or starboard as the situation demanded, constantly telling us to be looking, looking, looking. This was his refrain; looking looking, looking. He refused to go below and went without sleep for 36 hours. Nothing would persuade him that we could see the leads just as well as he. Eventually he collapsed and fell asleep across the chart table.

Clockwise from top left: *We met a fisherman, Alexander, who gave us a gift of fish; the remains of one of Stalin's Gulag prison camps; a collapsed Gulag watch tower.*

At 09.30 on 1 August Cape Vankarem was astern. Captain Bob Bartlett, the seasoned veteran of many polar expeditions, with his companion, the young Inuit Kataktovik, arrived ashore here in April 1914 after a hazardous crossing of the sea ice from Wrangel Island, and then sledged to Providenia Bay to seek assistance for the shipwrecked sailors of the *Karluk*.

As we made our way along the shore a small aluminium fishing boat came alongside and offered us some fish which we gratefully accepted. The fisherman told us his name was Alexander. He was a scientist based at Mys Schmidt, employed in the study of cosmic radiation. His fishing holiday was over and he offered to guide us there if we towed his boat. He was welcomed aboard and his local knowledge proved helpful. He pointed out the sights as we travelled along, weaving our way through ³⁄₁₀ ice.

The remains of a timber jetty ashore caught our attention. On learning that it was the landing stage for one of the notorious Far Northern Administration (Dolstroi) work camps (or Gulag) we landed to inspect the remains. The political prisoners built a road to the mines about 30km inland. Those who survived from the road building then mined the ore. They transported the ore to the jetty and loaded it on to ships. It was a most inhospitable place when we saw it in summer; how awful it must have been in the frozen winter. We left feeling a great sorrow for the injustice meted out to those innocent political prisoners.

Fog closed in as we neared Mys Schmidt and the ice became heavier. Our weaving became more pronounced as we tried to avoid the floating chunks of ice, occasionally crashing headlong into semi-submerged floes, making the off-watch crew in their bunks leap for their survival suits. Eventually we anchored in the early morning of 2 August at 03.00, 100 metres offshore, the fog almost obscuring the town.

Clockwise from top left: *Paddy at the memorial in Mys Schmidt to Captain Cook who sailed here in 1778; Michael and Rory strolling on the main street in Mys Schmidt, with military scrap metal in the background; our anchorage at Mys Schmidt.*

As in many Siberian towns, nearly all the military personnel had withdrawn; the new Russian Republic were unable or unwilling to pay their wages. For a final gesture the buildings were abandoned and wrecked. One apartment block in particular was particularly damaged; the windows were smashed and all the apartments' contents were thrown out, where it lay on the ground as a memorial to the disgruntled military men. Rusting military installations were everywhere; in the barracks we found reels of 32mm propaganda film.

Alexander showed us his laboratory, and his scientific data collection equipment. After the fall of the USSR, he was abandoned here like thousands of other workers, without wages for six months.

We were lucky to meet Urie, the airport manager, whose other main interest is local history. Through his efforts, a memorial to Captain James Cook was erected in the square. It is not generally known that Cook voyaged here in 1778 from the Pacific. Here he was stopped by pack ice, and this was his furthest west. The Russian yacht *Apostle Andrew* was also held up here for 25 days on its voyage through the North East Passage in 1998-1999. This was a reminder once again of how difficult sailing the North East Passage can be.

Though the weather was sunny and breezy now, the weather forecast and ice information on the route ahead was not favourable. As the wind increased, our anchor dragged. We moved *Northabout* into the lee of a grounded berg and moored to it with grapnels. This was more secure than at anchor where we were being bashed by ice-floes, drifting by at a speed of 1 knot. Raising the anchor was not easy; we had difficulty in retrieving the anchor and chain from under the floes.

Next day all the ice started to move with the wind and the high tide, including our 'secure' berg. Again we retrieved our grapnels and moved to another berg. This one was firmly aground and stayed put for the rest of our time in Mys Schmidt. That night we had a full moon, large and brilliant in the twilight. Cameras were out capturing the image.

Slava was in touch twice daily with the Murmansk Shipping Company on the satellite phone, reporting our position and getting ice reports. Conditions were not ideal, though to us there seemed no reason why we shouldn't be pushing on and getting as far west as possible. Slava used that Great Russian phrase, 'Big problem', when we suggested we should be on our way. This eventually led to a confrontation with Slava – exactly what was his role with us? Advisory or controller? He agreed he was in an advisory capacity, and after some heated discussion it was agreed we would leave the next morning at 06.00. We hoped he didn't know something he wasn't telling us.

Six of the crew had moved into the hotel, where they were living the high life and partying all night with some Ukranian building workers. This may be the reason why our planned departure at 06.00 didn't happen until 08.00 on 5 August.

Kevin is a keen observer of human nature; it is interesting to recall his observations of Slava, made in the early days of our voyage:

One of the conditions of our permit to sail the North East Passage is that we are accompanied

Slava and Paddy.

by an approved Russian ice pilot. Our pilot is Vladislav Lashkevic, who goes by the name of Slava.

Slava is 61 years old, grey haired with a splendid moustache, and is short and stout. He was born in Moscow and grew up in Siberia and has been an ice pilot for 23 years. When speaking he can become very animated with eloquent hand gestures and facial expressions. During an impromptu music session he stole the show by doing a Cossack-style dance on the deck, showing remarkable agility, with sinuous dance steps that would not be out of place at the Bolshoi.

We first met him in Moscow when he turned up in full uniform with black blazer resplendent, gold braid and buttons – and carrying an officious-looking briefcase. Now that he has settled aboard we seldom see the full regalia but it is very effective when dealing with the authorities when we have to call into poor, such as harbour masters, border guards and police.

Having a person such as Slava aboard a small boat like Northabout was a totally new experience to us. Compatibility of the group is vital on a voyage such as this and the introduction of an outsider has the potential to be very disruptive. Similarly, it must be extremely difficult for him, who is used to working on big ships among his fellow Russians, to find himself on a small boat among an eccentric bunch of Irishmen.

The principal source of potential friction is the interpretation of his responsibility and authority vis-a-vis that of our expedition leader and skipper. After a few fraught exchanges it is now accepted that his role is advisory and Northabout's leaders are the ultimate decision makers. However, we recognise that that his knowledge and experience of this area is immense. Consensus is always sought and mostly achieved.

We gave him the largest bunk out of deference to his position as ice pilot and his special relationship with us. You could see that his experience at sea had all been in big cargo boats from the way he hung his clothes on hangers around the bunk and arranged his toiletries alongside. We managed to explain to him that a more practical way of stowing his possessions was required, otherwise they would all be scattered with the first heavy seas.

He settled admirably into the boat routine and was very conscientious in making his regular radio reports to the Northern Sea administration officers in Murmansk and to ice breakers in our area. We were very fortunate in that he had good personal relations with the administration people and captains of the ice-breakers. This gave us a sense of confidence that the powers that be were always aware of our situation and the assurance that, as they were well disposed towards us, they would do their best to help us complete our voyage.

Slava had a great fondness for fish and on our infrequent visits ashore he would invariably return with a bagful of hard-to-identify specimens. He seemed to prefer his fish well hung which was a new experience for us. At one stage he proclaimed that he would cook a Russian dinner for us with slightly rancid fish as the centrepiece.

He chopped all day, muttering 'chopping, chopping, chopping' happily to himself – potatoes, assorted vegetables and, of course, the fish. He produced sauce bottles and herbs from under his bunk and simmered the lot in a big pot. The accompanying drink was, of course, a special bottle of vodka and the overall result was a splendid success.

His temperament was mostly placid but he could become very spirited if aroused.

He had some angry animated exchanges with the authorities on the radio and would continue muttering angrily to himself long after the call was over. We were never sure what the differences were about. He had his ups and downs with all of us too. However, it was noticeable that the further we got into the voyage the more comfortable our relationship became with him. When we had to overwinter the boat in Khatanga we had the opportunity to get a different pilot for the second year of our journey but we all opted to have Slava back again.

At times he could look very dispirited and withdrawn. I think he keenly noticed the many advantages we enjoy in our lives in Ireland compared to the hard conditions he had to endure in Russia. At one point he was reading an old Russian magazine and I saw him suddenly get very agitated, take up a pen and angrily scribble on the magazine page. I looked over and saw that he had obliterated the eyes of a smiling Boris Yeltsin. 'Bad man, bad man', he muttered. It turned out that Yeltsin had severely devalued the rouble and made Slava's life savings almost worthless. It was just another reminder to us of how lucky we are to be born in our own time and place.

In times of adversity he would remind us that 'the last thing to die is hope'.

He is devoutly religious and would pray openly every morning with much crossing of forehead, shoulders and breast.

We left him at Murmansk with much hugging and many toasts.

'Nastrovia' Slava, we will remember you fondly.

Kevin's insight and pacifying influence were crucial to keeping our common goal in focus.

At 10.45 we passed the 180-degree meridian line; we were now exactly halfway around the world from the prime meridian line at Greenwich. A remarkable steel sculpture marks the line ashore on the tundra. We celebrated this significant milestone and our viewing of it in our usual way – a little tot was issued to all.

The information we received in Mys Schmidt indicated ice conditions were poor until Billings Point, 111 miles distant. And so they were. With moderate ice and some fog we made good progress close inshore, following the coastline, travelling many more miles but avoiding the heavier pack ice. Slava spent his time in the cockpit advising us to be 'looking, looking, looking'.

After we passed Point Billings (named after the explorer, Captain Joseph Billings) the ice conditions improved, long leads opened up – 'the long mile road' as Gary called it. Gary took advantage of the improved conditions and filmed from the dinghy as we sailed by under full sail. Later, a beautiful rainbow appeared as we approached Pevek.

We tied up alongside an old sunken barge in Pevek Harbour on Saturday evening, 7 August.

The border guards were quickly aboard checking our papers. As before we were told of a 'big problem' with our documentation. Slava, his impressive gold braided uniform and wearing briefcase, with much shouting and arm waving, tried to outrank the border guards. Despite his smaller stature, Slava wasn't going to be beholden to these upstarts. Official uniforms carry a lot of weight in Russia – the more gold braid the better. Colm, too, was busy explaining that all our paperwork was in order and after posturing for a time the border guards stamped our papers and we were free to leave the boat.

Pevek was an impressive-looking port in the recent past. Now it is a sad sight, with docks crumbling, and its large cranes idle. The buildings likewise are falling derelict. Its population once 13,000, is now less than 2,000.

As *Northabout* was securely moored under the protection of an armed guard, we all went ashore for a meal and secured a couple of rooms in the hotel for showers. The hotel was basic but it had all our necessary requirements, a bed and a shower. Rory asked the hotel management to lower the room temperature but this wasn't possible. The entire town is on a communal heating system and everyone gets the same unregulated heat.

We were pleasantly surprised to find a good bar/restaurant, the Caf Romashka, where we had a fine meal.

Next day was spent at various activities: Paddy went hillwalking and was invited to join in a picnic

Top: *Apartments in Pevek.*
Left: *Pevek docks and cranes awaiting ships.*

party while others bought fresh food and did their laundry. I succeeded in purchasing diesel and water from a nearby vessel. In the afternoon Rory and Gary somehow got involved in a wedding party in the bar. When I arrived later in the evening they introduced me to their new friends, all speaking Russian fluently!

A great music session followed, ending up in an apartment in the early hours. Under the influence of vodka, we found we all had the gift of tongues and could speak Russian without any bother. Despite their difficult living conditions, the people we met couldn't have been more helpful or friendly; we were overwhelmed by our hosts' generosity. When I admired an ancient *samovar* (a heated vessel used throughout Russia for brewing tea), obviously a family heirloom, the good woman of the house wanted to give it to me as a gift! With difficulty I persuaded her I had no room aboard to take it.

We departed next day at 13.00 bound for Tiksi, 800 miles away

Say 'Cheese' Paddy

When it comes to cooking or snacking there is nothing as versatile and satisfying as cheese – be it with a cracker aboard in bad weather or in an omelette after an early morning shift. And what's an omelette without salt?

Can you imagine our horror when Tom Moran told us in Anadyr that the $338 worth of mild cheddar cheese and $22 worth of salt purchased in Prince Rupert could not be found aboard. We were assured a thorough search of the boat had been carried out.

Did you ever try buying cheddar cheese or salt in Siberia? However, we were not to be defeated in our quest of the elusive North East Passage by the mere lack of cheddar cheese and salt. Our spuds and vegetables were boiled in seawater. All our washing up was done in the same, giving us a good taste of the salt. As we braved our way north through the Bering Strait, on past Cape Dezhnev ▶

Say 'Cheese' Paddy.

and into the North East Passage, happily snacking on tinned sardines, tinned tuna, crackers and jam, etc. etc. the strain began to tell.

The skipper ordered another, even more thorough search for the missing essentials. Kevin searched his area, Paddy his, Colm his and so on, and all reported negative. We were to be resigned to the hardships of our expedition without these basic comforts but we would 'sailor' on.

Life aboard continued as normal. Six crew operate three-hour shifts around the clock. Cameraman Gary Finnegan and ice pilot Slava rotated freely.

Somehow, Paddy decided that he would carry out an inventory of all foods in his compartment for no apparent reason. Kevin and Rory and myself were bemused [and ready with cameras] when he sheepishly appeared at his door holding three fine blocks of mild cheddar cheese and a box of salt. We happily feasted on omelettes with cheese and salt as we sailed west into a force six North Westerly. Heaven!

Michael Brogan

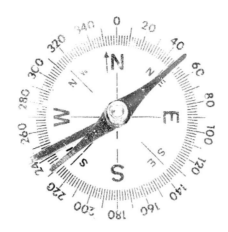

14

PEVEK TO TIKSI

Sunday 8 August we departed Pevek at 13.00. As we sailed out of the harbour with all crew sitting in the cockpit, we discussed the events in Pevek, imagining the reaction of the locals if seven Russian sailors arrived into Kiltimagh. We were all glad to be on our way.

The wind from the northwest was cold; all were wearing full 'battle dress', and progress was good. Today we made clear radio contact with Brendan. His weather forecasts indicated the winds would swing to the south for four days, which would be a favourable sailing wind and would help keep the ice away from the shore.

On Monday, we had dense fog, cold rain in the face, sometimes heavy ice, sometimes lighter, a typical Siberian day. By 15.15 Cape Baranov was abeam. 140 miles had been covered in the direct line from Pevek, not too bad considering the conditions.

Next day brought an improvement, with light wind and no ice. We were motor sailing at 8 knots and making good progress. The sea has shallow banks here and we were keeping close to the 4-metre depth contour. Michael cooked a very civilised dinner of Pevek caribou steaks, which was enjoyed in the cockpit in the sunny evening.

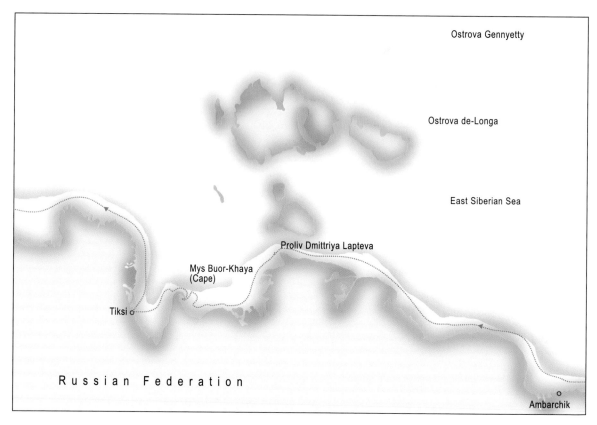

Pevek to Tiksi.

On Wednesday 11 August and the following days, the log entry told of our frustration, and how we were back to Siberian weather again. The wind was from dead ahead, unlike that forecasted. Our speed in the lumpy sea was reduced to 3.5-4 knots; dodging ice growlers, cold wet sea in the face. A minor disaster today was that we lost our bucket when its handle broke. The bucket was used to scoop seawater aboard for washing up. By late evening the sea and wind had calmed but ice was heavier, slowing our progress. We are skirting the ice; this involves long detours, increasing our mileage.

Thursday 12 August: we sighted the icebreaker *Borudkin* and a convoy of three ships heading east. Slava spoke with them – their ice report was not encouraging; 6/10 ice on the direct route to Tiksi. We thought that perhaps better conditions might be found close inshore. They also reported that conditions from Tiksi to Chelyuskin were bad, and the Kara Sea almost clear. It sounded like we might be in Tiksi for a while, but if we could get around Cape Chelyuskin we will be on the home strait.

At 16.00 we left the East Siberian Sea and entered the Laptev Sea, through the 25-mile wide Demetri Laptev Strait, between M Syvatoy Nos on the mainland and Lyahovskiy Island to the north. This was another significant milestone on our route.

Getting through the strait was difficult, with much heavy ice; we had to break a path through ice that seemed impenetrable. Once through, our route now was to the appropriately named headland of Mys Buor Khaya, meaning, 'Big Nose', a common name worldwide for headlands. The direct route there is 153 miles, though many more miles were going to be logged because of diversions and retreating from blind alleys. Frequently, we had to retreat a couple of miles, when the lead we had chosen turned out to be impassable. To give up those hard fought miles was frustrating, but Kevin sums it up nicely in his log entry quoting an Irish proverb 'It is better to return from the middle of the ford than to drown in the flood.'

Friday 13 August: an ominous day for superstitious sailors. Nevertheless we made good progress initially, through ice and fog, which forced us to follow the coastline into Yansky Bay.

At midday we were forced to retreat back the way we came for about 30 miles, as there seemed to be no way through the heavy pack ice. At 15.15 we broke out of the ice. Although we could see ice ahead, we were now only 35 miles from Buor Khaya; the icebreaker said we should find clear water on the 6-metre contour.

Saturday 14 August: on this day we found ourselves with ice ahead, ice each side and ice behind us! We seemed to be trapped in the bay with no way out. For several hours we were going around in circles seeking a way forward. There seemed to be no way out.

At 0600 we finally anchored in 2.3 metre depth, in bight south of Buor Khaya point. The last couple of days had taken their toll; everyone was worn out, and in need of rest. The wind was

Rory entertaining the crew.

Ice-breaker emerging through the fog.

north- easterly force 3 to force 4, with cold rain. The low spit to the north was barely visible; thankfully it kept our bay clear of ice, enabling all to catch up on sleep. The lighthouse on the point was occasionally visible in breaks in the driving rain. Nevertheless, all was snug on board. After a rest the crew enjoyed a good dinner, followed by a music session to keep the spirits up.

During the night the wind increased to force 6 with driving rain.

Sunday 15 August: we were still at anchor. Thankfully it was a better day. The skies were grey, but there was no rain. We could now see the spit, which was protecting us from the pack ice to the north. The ice-breaker *Borukin* reported that the route to Tiksi was blocked inshore; the only slight possibility of getting through was on the 5-metre depth contour.

Rory called our anchorage 'impatience bay'. It was a name that neatly expressed our mood at this point.

Monday 16 August: we raised anchor at 06.30. The wind had dropped to a light northerly, foggy with poor visibility of 50 metres. The good news on that day was that there was an ice-breaker coming from the east. As we moved out of the shelter of the spit we were again back into 3/10 ice, which became heavier, 6/10, as we made our way north to deeper water. By 11.00 having tried every lead and re-traced our tracks many times, we could go no further. We were totally surrounded by heavy ice, with no way out. We were drifting with the ice to the north at 0.3 knots, a small consolation, but even this didn't last. Our drift reversed to the south, perhaps caused by the tide. At midday we started the engine and tried again to force our way north; the leads seemed to be slightly better, but after two hours of pushing and banging ice we had to admit defeat. We were going nowhere, and there was ice all around. Visibility in the fog was about 200 metres. The depth of water was 12.4 metres.

At 16.30 we spoke with the ice-breaker *Kapitan Babich* now only 3 miles away, leading a convoy of ships travelling westward toward us. We asked Slava to talk to the Captain and ask if we could join the convoy. To this simple request we couldn't get a straight answer; 'maybe' was the best answer we could get from him. However, he did ask us to try to get to the 10-metre depth contour, along which the icebreaker was travelling. With great difficulty and with a lot of crashing, pushing and poling the ice we got to the 10 metre line, about 2 miles offshore. There we waited, not knowing whether we would be allowed to join in the convoy, or be run down by the icebreaker.

At 20.00 the icebreaker came crashing through the ice 100 metres off our port side, invisible in the fog until within 100 metres. We needn't have worried; they saw us on radar from a long way off. We were instructed to take our position behind the fifth and last vessel.

This was not so easily done as we were still surrounded by ice, but we did succeed. With the engine on full power, we pushed the ice aside and took up position behind the tanker, *Lena Oil*. The convoy was travelling at 4.1 knots; we had no difficulty in keeping up with them at that speed. Surprisingly the entire convoy was weaving through the ice. I expected the icebreaker would break a straight path through everything in its path, but no, they take the line of least resistance, and avoid the heaviest ice.

By 22.00 Buor Khaya was left well behind us, visibility improved, fog disappeared and the ice took on a golden glow in the evening sun. The crew of the vessel ahead of us gathered at their stern to listen to Michael and Gary play a few tunes – they must have thought that these seamen were crazed from their time marooned in the ice.

After 40 miles the ice thinned out, and the convoy's speed increased to 7.5 knots.

Tuesday 17 August, 02.00: we were almost out of the ice, with only isolated growlers visible, as we broke away from the convoy. We now set our course directly for Tiksi, with the convoy going

Left to right: *In convoy, Michael and Gary entertain the Russian ship's crew; Rory collecting ice to melt for fresh water.*

From top: Campina *leaving Tiksi; Tiksi; Rory in Tiksi museum with artefacts from the* Jeanette *disaster.*

to the Lena river. We gave a warm salute to Slava, and three cheers for the captain of *Kapitan Babich* without whom we couldn't have got around Buor Khaya.

Tiksi was in sight at 09.00, and by 11.00 (local time 08.00) we had tied up alongside at the wooden dock. The morning was bright and sunny; we were all in high spirits and looking forward to showers and some time ashore, after the rigours of the past week.

The docks at Tiksi are extensive; I counted 22 cranes, only two of them in working order. Tiksi is the major shipping port in this region, but now in serious decline. I seem to be repeating myself every time I try to describe the towns in Siberia. The population was reported to have dropped from 15,000 to 3,000. There were no ships in port while we were there. The only vessels apart from ourselves were a small immobile navy boat with its propeller on the aft deck, and the Dutch yacht *Campina.* Henk de Veld, the skipper, was attempting the North East Passage, and had got as far as Tiksi the previous year but because of heavy ice ahead he had decided to over-winter in Tiksi. Unlike us who were fully crewed he was sailing single-handed, if one does not count Boris, his mandatory ice-pilot.

After the entry formalities, which were as tedious as in previous ports, we took a walk around town seeking the highlights, which we failed to find. We did succeed in arranging to have dinner ashore in a restaurant, and arranged to have a sauna (*banya*) next day. Slava had previously lived in Tiksi and met up with some of his old friends and disappeared for the duration of our time ashore. Before leaving, there was much work to be done. I serviced the engine and changed oil and filters, while others organised a diesel fill, topped up the water tank, and re-stocked with food. In town we visited the museum, which had many artefacts of the native people – the Dolgan, and of interest to us, had a section on the ill-fated American vessel the *Jeannette,* which was lost in ice on its polar expedition in 1881. Some of the survivors succeeded in reaching land near here, only to die of starvation in the wilderness.

15

TIKSI TO TAYMYR PENINSULA

On Friday 20 August at 11.15 we cast off our lines and departed from Tiksi with no regrets. We were happy to arrive there two days previously but two days was enough time in that run-down town. On the other hand Slava, had been having a great time with his old buddies and was reluctant to leave. Kevin eventually succeeded in getting him on board, with his tact and persuasion. *Campina* had also left earlier that morning after a goodbye ceremony on the dock. Henk de Velde, her skipper, having spent the winter in Tiksi, had a group of well wishers and ourselves to see him off.

We stopped near the Lena Delta and held a ceremony in remembrance of Jerome Collins, Captain DeLong and the crew of the *Jeanette* who lost their lives in this inhospitable region. Kevin cast a wreath of local flowers into the sea as we said a short prayer in memory of their tragic fate.

Campina contacted us by radio. Her skipper had a problem with leaking cooling water and needed some water hose, which we were able to give him when we met later.

For the next couple of days we made good progress in easy-going favourable weather. Sometimes it was sunny, sometimes foggy, with light following winds and occasionally a few ice floes to keep the helmsman on his guard. *Campina* did not make radio contact as agreed, a situation we understood

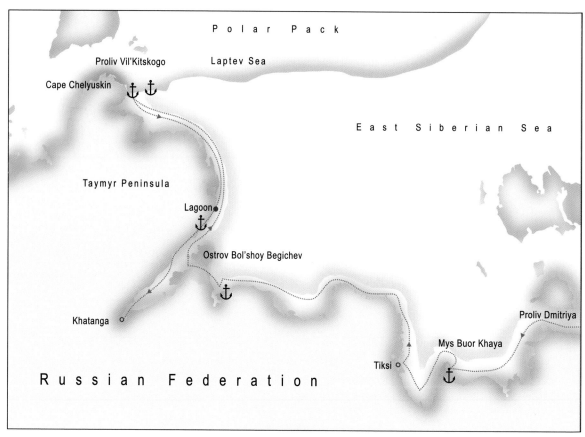

Above: *Tiksi to Taymyr Peninsula; the anchor symbols indicate locations where we were stopped for a time by ice. The grey shaded area indicates approximately the impenetrable pack ice.*

Right: *We laid a wreath on the sea in memory of Jerome Collins and all who lost their lives in the Jeanette disaster.*

Above: *Kevin going for a swim at Mys Lygyy.*
Left: *The tanker was also icebound nearby.*

only too well – Henk being short crewed, he probably had enough to do on his first days at sea.

Off the headland of Mys Lygyy, we encountered heavy ice, which stopped all progress.

We spoke on the radio with the tanker, *Kaptin Sdoboshion*, which was anchored nearby. They were waiting for an ice-breaker to take them through the 4.5-mile wide Vostochnyy Strait, south of Begichev Island. As this was our route too, we decided to wait – in fact, we had no choice. We were ice-bound!

As we waited in beautiful sunshine, we spent time photographing the amazing ice formations and admiring the delicate light blue and green hues of the ice in the cold sea. There was something tempting about this sea; soon the hardier crew members decided it was time for a swim. Paddy, Rory, Colm and Kevin plunged into the icy sea for about the same duration as the camera shutter speed, 1/125 second. I never saw people get out of the water so fast. Our doctor forbade any further swimming; he didn't have any facilities for dealing with cardiac arrest!

Northabout *in ice*.

Since we were ice-bound, we secured *Northabout* to a floe from Sunday midnight until Monday night. After a lovely calm, sunny day, the weather changed for the worse. The easterly wind increased to force 4, pressing the ice around us. It also brought cold rain. At 22.00, in the middle of a card game, the tanker called us, saying they were concerned for their safety and were trying to get out of the ice. They advised us to follow them. We reasoned that if they were concerned then we too were in danger. The ice at this stage had tightened its grip on *Northabout* and if the pressure increased further we were in danger of being crushed. We decided to follow the tanker; they should be able to clear a path for us to follow.

The card game was quickly abandoned and foul-weather clothing donned. Pushing aside ice floes, with the engine at full revs, we motored behind the tanker as it started to weave its way through the ice.

The tanker was a twin propeller vessel and when it needed to turn, power was applied to port or starboard propeller as needed. This made it impossible for us to remain in the central protected position behind, as we were being pushed to port or starboard by the propeller wash. In the propeller wash we were hammered by huge chunks of ice driven at speed onto our hull. No matter how hard we tried we couldn't stay directly behind the tanker – any of those chunks was capable of holing *Northabout*.

The tanker crew, seeing our predicament, stopped and lowered a tow rope, which we secured to our bow. Off we went again, and now the rope kept our bow safely between the propeller streams. Occasionally the tanker had to reverse to avoid an iceberg. When this was about to happen they would signal us with their siren and we would engage reverse to avoid being run over. These were the most terrifying hours of our entire voyage.

Northabout was being bashed by huge chunks of ice flying back from the tanker's propellers; the sound of the impacts was frightening. I wondered could the hull stand much more of this abuse. A particularly hard collision on the starboard side brought Rory out of his bunk and into his survival suit, ready to abandon ship. The dents on the hull remain as a reminder of that night. On our deck a crewman stood ready to cut the tow should it become necessary. We expected a short tow to the ice edge but, finding that ice had accumulated to the east, the tanker decided the quickest way out of the ice was through Vostochnny Strait, 27 miles to the northwest.

Eventually, after twelve hours of hard bashing, we rounded Cape Paksa and arrived into improved ice conditions. By evening we were out of the ice and the tow rope was at last released. We said goodbye to our new friends, having given them a cash donation and a bottle of Irish whiskey for the care they had taken of us.

We were all exhausted and in need of sleep so we anchored for the night under the cliffs near Cape Goristyy in 6 metres depth. The calm evening was exactly what we needed to catch up on our rest. The hull had developed a leak somewhere forward; as the pumps were capable of dealing with the flow, there was no immediate worry.

Paddy and Michael, who skippered wooden boats, were unperturbed by a leak, being hardened by constant pumping of their craft. I, on the other hand, was more concerned – metal boats shouldn't leak!

In the morning we lifted the floorboards and found the leak at the depth-sounder transducer, probably from being hit by ice. In a way this was a relief; the welding had survived intact! Nothing could be done at the moment; we needed to dry out the hull ashore

Top: *The tanker's propeller wash drives huge pieces of ice at speed into our hull.*
Above: *We sustained damage from the ice and had to pump out the bilges to stay afloat.*

to see the full extent of the damage. With the engine driven 2-inch bilge pump we should be able to keep the water pumped out until the repair was done.

We got underway at 10.15 and were soon in ice again. Unfortunately, we could get nowhere in this closely packed ice. We retraced our way to Cape Goristyy and anchored again. Later in the day we tried heading north again and this time found a lead close inshore. With centreboard raised, we made our way cautiously along the shore and by evening we had rounded Cape Tsvetkov.

On the ice we saw a huge walrus and on the shore we saw an adult polar bear, an old male – our first sighting in Siberia. We made our way to within 45 metres of him, with all cameras taking photographs. Slava became agitated, explaining that the bear could easily outpace us in water or on land. Luckily the bear showed no interest in us and shuffled away.

Shortly after midnight on Thursday 26 August, we encountered heavy polar pack ice which stopped any further progress. Despite the difficult conditions though, we had travelled 68 miles in the day. We anchored for the night. In the morning conditions were no better, with heavy ice all around.

There had still been no radio contact with *Campina*, although we were trying to keep to the agreed radio schedule. Finally, through our radio contact with the icebreaker *Viagach*, we got news of him. *Campina* had engine trouble and was now with a convoy in roughly the same position as where we had been stuck in the ice four days earlier.

We go ashore and climb the cliffs to get a better view of ice conditions ahead; we found these tundra flowers.

Clockwise from top: *Paddy climbing the mast to see if there is any way through the ice ahead; having beached* Northabout, *Paddy tunnels under the hull to get at the source of the leak; a view of the lagoon where we beached* Northabout *and lit a fire for a barbecue ashore.*

It was late evening before the ice opened up and then only slightly. The weather was bitterly cold, a force 6 biting wind from the northwest, with sleet. The hull leak was worse, every four hours we pumped for nearly an hour. We were looking for a suitable bay where we could repair the damage.

At 20.30 we were again stopped by ice. Though we could see clear water ahead, a barrier of heavy ice one mile wide stopped all progress. The distance travelled all that day was a mere 12 miles.

This was one of the lowest points of our voyage; we were stopped by ice, our boat was leaking, we were far from assistance and even the weather forecast was bad. In my mind were thoughts of spending winter beset in the ice like the explorers of old. Why hadn't we taken the more pleasant option of sailing home through the Panama Canal and the colourful Caribbean Islands?

Ashore there was nothing to brighten the scene either, only endless miles of uninhabited, undulating, boggy tundra. A group of us went ashore to climb the higher ground and see ice conditions ahead. We startled an Arctic fox in his new white winter coat; he obviously knew the winter was about to arrive (in winter, Arctic foxes abandon their brown summer fur coat for white camouflage fur).

From the cliffs there was no open water visible anywhere. But we did see a small lagoon, at the mouth of a stream, which might be suitable for beaching our leaking craft. Having checked that the depths were sufficient by dinghy, we entered Kul'dina Lagoon and beached *Northabout* at the top of the tide. As we waited for the water to recede, we gathered driftwood, built a bonfire and had a barbecue ashore, keeping a wary eye out for the hungry polar bear. At low water Paddy, in his drysuit, tunnelled under the hull to access the damaged area.

From inside the hull I removed the depth sounder and, sure enough, found the source of the leak; the transducer flange was cracked and the gasket split. Not having a spare transducer or gasket on board, I had to improvise; with the doctor's scalpel I cut a new gasket using the material from an old rubber boot. With lots of mastic sealant spread liberally, the transducer was replaced. To remove the transducer, it was necessary to cut the wires leading to it. Not wanting to be without depth information, Rory soldered the wires and then encapsulated them in epoxy resin to prevent corrosion. As *Northabout* re-floated, we were delighted to find the repair was a complete success – the leak was fixed and the depth sounder also worked!

As an added bonus while in the lagoon, we found a stream of really clean water and topped up our water tank. This was the first occasion where we had got clean water in Russia.

On Saturday 28 August at 13.00, we headed north again, the ice having opened up a little. We crept cautiously along the shore. By 21.00 we had crossed the significant 76-degree north line, the furthest north we had been.

Four hours later we were stopped again by a solid mass of heavy polar pack ice. We were up against the proverbial brick wall. There was no way forward, inshore or offshore. At 01.00 next morning, we anchored at 76°.15 N with fast shore ice ahead.

Our total mileage for the day was 53 miles. New ice was forming in the sea.

The temperature dropped to minus 5 degrees. The Irish tricolour on our stern was frozen solid.

The only good news was that we had only 150 miles to go to Cape Chelyuskin (Proliv Vil'kitskogo) the most northerly point of mainland Russia. After that, the sea would be ice free.

On Sunday 29 August conditions were cold, with light snow in a north-easterly wind. We tried to get out to deeper water where we might join the next west-going convoy. At 14.50 we moored to ice off the southern tip of Yuzhnny Island, in 12 metres depth.

We had a radio link up on short wave radio to listen to the All-Ireland football semi-final match. Mayo won! We were ecstatic – at least the Mayo crew were! Rory was the most ardent fan and

The Mayo team!

went to great lengths to hear the radio transmission. To celebrate the win, we had a football game on the ice. We used a round fender as a football and Rory proudly wore his red and green Mayo football jersey. As a memento for Rory, Gary made a photo-montage of us all wearing the Mayo jersey. Since we only had one jersey, Gary photographed each of us in turn wearing the jersey and then manipulated the digital image to show all eight of us in the Mayo colours as a team on the ice. The digital camera *can* lie!

A young polar bear then visited us; he came too close for comfort. Rory describes the scene in more graphic detail:

A Visit from Nanook

It was Friday 3 September 2004. The time on Northabout's *clock said 17.00 but locally it was about 21.00.*

We had just come to the end of a very tasty spam curry and were settling down to a hot drink and a bit of social interaction. We had been at anchor for six days now and most of that time was spent in our bunks – each man listening to his Walkman and reading in his own little cocoon. The only time we all got together was for the evening meal and it was like men coming out of a trance. The talk started slowly, moved a little quicker, and by the time the meal was on the table it was hard to get a word in sideways. There wasn't a whole lot of

We had seen a bear a week earlier but it had just sat motionless as we took photographs.

current news to discuss but we usually had somebody telling a good yarn, from the old country.

Kevin got up to put on the kettle and something outside caught his eye. He had a better look and then called 'polar bear' as he darted towards his bunk to get his camera. Everyone leapt into action, grabbing cameras. We had seen a bear a week earlier but I had just sat motionless as we took photographs. It was on the tundra shore, with mud all around him, and it wasn't the ideal background for us budding 'National Geographic photographers'. This time, on the other hand, was a world devoid of mud – we were anchored off the pack ice – and it could not have been better.

We clambered out on deck (my first time that day) and were greeted by the awesome sight of a beautiful polar bear just coming out of the water (about 20 metres from the boat). I watched as he effortlessly stepped up the ice floe and shook his fur. I remember thinking that there must be steps cut in the ice, he moved so freely. My mind was full of shutter speeds and film speeds – as it was almost dusk – and while we could see him clearly, the cameras might not deal with the low light so well. I was now just becoming aware of the cold night air. He stood and stared at us for a few seconds, his nose twitching and his neck reaching skywards – I am not sure how many times he has registered the smell of spam curry! He then started to move towards us with a very balanced gait. Not a run but certainly not anything hesitant either.

Looking through the lens, I fired off frame after frame – until he was completely filling my viewfinder. At that stage, I looked up from the camera, to see that the bear was only 5 metres or so from the boat.

What had started off as good-natured banter now changed to nervous giggling and a sense that 'this was fine, let's stop it now'. Gary kept filming as we all moved in and out of the cabin. I moved down to get more clothing, as it was now freezing (I had been on deck for only about five minutes). Jarlath, as always – thinking ahead – had brought up some emergency flares from below. Although we had tried to get a gun in Anadyr, our attempts were unsuccessful – and in the weeks since, we had discussed loosely what we would do if we encountered polar bears.

'Stand back!' called Jarlath as he held the flare out in his left hand and pulled the cord with his right. There was a fizzling sound like an Alka Seltzer in water – but alas, no bright red light!

While this was happening, I remember staring at the bear (advice says not to make eye contact) and my eyes being drawn to his claws. Even though this bear was small – in bear terms – his claws were each about the length of my fingers – and the sharp black claws stood out in stark relief against the ice on which he stood. For all the cuddly appearance of a young polar bear – and they do appear so nice – one look at his claws and the cuddly turns to a chilling killing machine.

While Jarlath's flare (we found out later that it was out of date) hissed, and we waited, hoping that it might still ignite – Mick Brogan called out to 'make as much noise as you can'. I got the ice pick and others got the timbers we use for poling through the ice – and we started to bang these against Northabout's aluminium structure. The noise seemed to disturb the bear and he moved back a metre or so. We upped the tempo but he again

moved towards the bow of the boat. He reached out and touched the side of the boat but recoiled, as if he hadn't expected it to be so hard, and we banged even louder. He started to move away but kept looking over his shoulder. After about four or five minutes, he had moved away to the edge of the ice and was back in the water, swimming in the direction from which he had come.

When we were satisfied he was gone, we all went below and began the 'what if' scenario. We knew we were lucky he had decided to move away. We were lucky he was on his own, we were lucky he was not aggressive and we were lucky he did not appear too hungry. If he had decided to attack us, we all knew that our hatchway was only a token defence.

We agreed that as soon as possible – we would get a gun!

Polar Bear (*Ursus Maritimus*) Nanuq by Michael Brogan

They are the largest of all bears, with males weighing up to 600kg, and stand 3.5 metres from nose to tail. They are almost entirely carnivorous, with seal meat comprising 90 per cent of their diet. But they occasionally eat walrus, beluga and narwhal. Mating occurs in spring but because of delayed implantation, the embryo does not begin to develop until September. In winter the female excavates a snow den where she remains dormant until her cubs, usually twins, are born in late November to January. The global population numbers 20,000 to 30,000. Hunting is strictly regulated. Indigenous people harvest 500-900 each year in subsistence hunts. Trichinosis, a parasitic worm found in polar bear meat, can be transferred to humans when it is under cooked. Many of the early explorers found to their cost that the level of vitamin A in the liver is toxic to humans. The fur provides excellent insulation, each hair being hollow. It is widely used by the northern Greenlanders to make trousers.

Polar bears are extremely strong swimmers, capable of swimming up to 60km. The first bear we saw in northern Greenland was cooling itself on an iceberg, 40 km from land. They spend most of their time hunting on sea ice. They either move onto the land in summer or move northward to the permanent multi-year ice. They have a keen sense of smell and sight, as we found out when we were stuck for eleven days in ice, east of the Taymyr peninsula.

The polar bear inspires both fear and respect in many northern communities and it is regarded as human in appearance and intelligence. When stalking seals, a bear will often cover its black nose with its paw, or with snow, to make it less visible. In Siberia, the population of bears was reduced from 20,000 to 10,000 in the 1950s and 1960s as a result of nuclear testing. Although the population is recovering since the 1970s, the biggest threat to the polar bear is the destruction of its habitat through global warming. If the sea ice disappears it will not be able to hunt successfully and will starve.

On the subject of bears, in Canada we were advised that some hunters wear small bells attached to their clothing to scare bears when in bear country: 'You will know you are in bear country when you see small bells in droppings.'

Slava spoke with the crew of the ice-breaker, *Viagach*, which had escorted *Campina* to within 25 miles south of our position. We could not get any real information from Slava, who liked to keep us in the dark. The only information we got was that *Viagach* was leaving *Campina* secured to a floe and then going north to have a look at ice conditions.

There we waited, sometimes moving when leads appeared but not really getting anywhere. On Wednesday *Viagach* reported the polar pack ice was too heavy for small craft like ours to follow them and recommended we stay where we were for five days.

That evening the ice started to move down on us in the northerly wind, a very dangerous situation. We moved to the shelter of nearby Vos'moye Marta Island and anchored in 2.6 metres in ice-free water.

On Thursday 2 September, the wind veered to the south force 5, forcing us to move to the other side of the island. On Saturday the wind shifted again to north-westerly, forcing us to move back to anchor off Yuzhnny Island.

Young ice forming.

A view of the hummocked heavy polar pack ice which stopped all progress forward. Colm, Michael and Kevin exercise on the ice.

The reports from Slava's conversation with the Murmansk shipping company were not encouraging – the sea off Chelyuskin was freezing up and it sounded like the shipping season was over for that year. We considered all our options on where to winter or whether we should look for a sealift on an ice-breaker.

Henk De Velde called to tell us that *Campina's* rudders were damaged and that his voyage was over. On Monday 7 September we recorded our lowest temperature – minus 8 degrees. The rudder was frozen solid, and there was some snow on deck. With the wind-chill factor it felt incredibly cold. After waiting ten days we were going nowhere. We wondered to ourselves if it was time to be on our way out of there.

A call from *Viagach* settled the matter. *Campina* needed a tow,

16

ASSISTANCE TO CAMPINA
AND WINTER LAY-UP
IN KHATANGA

As mentioned earlier, *Northabout* was not the only yacht attempting the North East Passage in 2004.

The Dutchman, Henk de Velde, had started the passage from the Bering Straits in 2003 in *Campina* and got as far as Tiksi. Because of reports of heavy ice ahead he decided to overwinter in Tiksi harbour. Henk is a very experienced and resourceful sailor, having three single-handed circumnavigations to his credit. He was completing his last-minute preparations for departure when we sailed into Siberia's Tiksi harbour.

Henk described to us being frozen-in for ten months in Tiksi harbour, 300 metres from shore. As the ice solidified and started to squeeze the hull, he cut a pressure-relieving channel around *Campina* with a chainsaw. Later, as ice re-formed from the bottom up, *Campina* was pushed upwards out of its icy prison. Henk had spent a cold, lonely winter living aboard in freezing conditions. Later on, I wondered if his subsequent engine problems resulted from ice damage sustained during that bitter Siberian winter.

Like us, he was anxious to be on his way and he put to sea a couple of hours ahead of *Northabout* on 20 August 2004. With fond farewells and radio schedule agreed, he waved goodbye. His final words were 'I leave Tiksi with a heavy heart but I won't look back'. Little did Henk or we know that he would indeed see Tiksi again very soon.

It is interesting to note that Gilbert Caroff designed both *Northabout* and *Campina*. While there is a family resemblance, both vessels are quite different. The larger *Campina* is 17 metres long, displaces 26 tons, and has a centreboard and twin rudders. *Northabout* is smaller, at 15 metres long, displaces 16 tons and draws 1.4 metres with centreboard raised. A shallow keel protects the rudder and propeller. *Northabout's* most distinctive feature is its raised 'ice-breaker style' bow. Polar travel in small craft involves much sailing in shallow water; the lifting centreboard design keeps the draft to the minimum and gives good sailing performance when lowered.

Northabout was fully crewed by seven hardy Irishmen and Slava, in contrast to *Campina*, which was sailed just by Henk and his ice pilot, Boris. Both our ice pilots were provided by the Murmansk Shipping Company, a mandatory requirement for sailing in Russian waters. Boris, a sprightly 72-year-old retired ice pilot, was clearly not happy with his shorthanded vessel. Henk was clearly determined to do this voyage single-handed, as in his previous voyages. But we considered that one

Northabout *and* Campina *anchored together.*

The evening after departure from Tiksi, Campina *sails into the sunset.*

has to be prepared to keep pushing on at every opportunity and so a big crew would be a necessity.

On the night following our departure we had a VHF radio call from *Campina*. Henk reported a problem with leaking engine-cooling water and needed some water hose. When we had rendezvoused we gave him a short length of 50mm hose.

Later, as we made our way up the Taymyr peninsula, we made radio contact with the patrolling ice-breaker *Vaigach*, 100 miles south of our position. We learned from them that *Campina*, further south, had reported a problem with her steering mechanism. *Vaigach* engineers assisted with the repairs.

By Tuesday 31 August we could make no further progress northwards. We moved and re-anchored as the wind changed, sometimes off Vos'Moye Marta Island and later off Yushnyy Island, constantly dodging the drifting ice floes. At this latitude a safe location can change in moments to a precarious one. For example, on one occasion, we narrowly avoided being crushed between the fast-ice and a drifting iceberg. On another occasion, as we lay moored to an ice floe, we had another narrow escape when suddenly two car-sized chunks of ice slid out from under the floe, narrowly missing *Northabout*.

Eventually *Campina* made direct radio contact with us. She had moored 25 miles south of our position. The engineers of the icebreaker *Vaigach* had rebuilt her cooling-water pump and their

Top: *Ice beginning to build up on our anchor chain, forming from the darker grease ice.* Right: Northabout *is struggling to tow* Campina *through newly-formed young ice.*

divers had repaired the ice-damaged steering mechanism. We spoke with *Vaigach* as it made its way to assist a convoy. We had hoped to travel behind *Vaigach* but they told us that the polar pack ahead was too heavy for small craft. They instructed us to wait and stay in contact. In the meantime, *Campina* planned to come to our position and we would both join the next north-going convoy. During the next two days we moved position several times to avoid drifting ice as the wind changed. A solid band of polar pack ice was still preventing any further northward progress. We settled down to await the break-up of the pack ice, which historically occurs here in the first weeks of September.

On Saturday 4 September we received a radio call from *Campina*. Henk announced with regret that his journey was over. As he lay moored to an iceberg, a drifting floe had crashed into his yacht.

His rudders had been irreparably damaged by ice. Fortunately, he was in no immediate danger. Arrangements had been made by radio with his sponsor, who was arranging a sealift for Henk and *Campina* on a Russian freighter.

Vaigach requested that we stand by *Campina* and tow her to deeper water. The reason for this request was that the ice-breaker operates in a minimum depth of 14 metres. She could not reach *Campina's* shallow water location. We agreed readily and made preparations to go to her assistance in the early morning, when the wind was forecast to ease.

On Sunday, as we lay anchored off Yushnyy Island, the weather took a turn for the worse, the temperature dropping to minus 7° Celsius. A freezing north-west wind with occasional snow flurries made the deck dangerous to walk on. Already the first signs of the formation of new sea ice were becoming visible with the development of small needle-like crystals known as frazil ice. This gives the sea an oily appearance. The next stage, which followed quickly, was the formation of grease ice. As its name suggests, this forms a greasy, soupy layer giving the sea a matte appearance. By 03.00 we discovered that our rudder was jammed with ice. The anchor chain too was coated in a thick layer of ice. We freed the rudder by chipping at the ice that was within our reach and by using the propeller wash to clear the rest. Raising the anchor was a struggle, almost freezing the hands of the anchor-raising party.

Grease ice 100mm thick slowed our progress as we motored south to *Campina*, bringing our speed down to less than 3 knots. *Campina* had moored to a grounded large ice floe (known as *sta-muga* in Russian) in shallow water. Henk agreed that we should tow him two miles to deeper water

The 44,000 horsepower nuclear ice-breaker, Viagach.

where the cargo ship would be able to pick him up. By 07.00 *Campina* was in sight but a band of heavy ice thwarted our approach from the north. We retreated and tried to find a route further offshore. By 10.15 and approaching from the east, we were again within sight of *Campina* but yet another band of heavy ice 400 metres wide lay between us. No amount of pushing floes and strenuous poling would allow us through. We consulted with *Vaigach* and were instructed to wait as they were on the way to assist. The icebreaker appeared later that evening. What an awesome sight – over 151 metres long, 44,000 HP and displacing 21,000 tonnes. Her 171-megawatt nuclear reactor was silent; *Vaigach* was without the usual ship's smoke plume. We fell in behind her as she made short work of the ice, proceeding slowly as far as she dared go into shallower water. With the all-seeing thermal imaging technology on board her high bridge, her skipper directed us to a lead through the remaining ice band.

When we reached *Campina* we found that she had been squeezed by a large drifting ice floe, which crushed her against the floe to which she was moored. Her vulnerable twin rudders were both bent and jammed against the hull and the hydraulic steering mechanism was also damaged. So *Campina* could not be steered and was virtually uncontrollable. Darkness was closing in, so we lost no time in getting a towrope attached and recovered the mooring lines. Cautiously, *Northabout* took the strain with the heavier *Campina* sheering uncontrollably to port. By adjusting the towing bridle, some semblance of control was established, though our speed was a mere 2 knots.

At this stage Slava, sprang a rather unpleasant surprise on us. He had been in radio contact with *Vaigach*, which had now moved north again, and he had agreed to their instruction that we should tow *Campina* south to a position off Psov Island, a distance of nearly 30 miles. In normal ice-free waters this would have been a reasonable request but the prospect of attempting a long tow in the ice-strewn conditions was daunting, to say the least. We were annoyed that we hadn't been consulted; we would have welcomed an opportunity to participate in the discussions with *Vaigach*. Slava didn't take kindly to our questioning his judgement. Not for the first time we found communications trying in Russia!

In the darkness we moored both boats for the night to a large floe. We invited Henk and Boris aboard for dinner, with the intention of resuming the tow at 07.00 in the morning. The night was calm with a beautiful sunset, the sea reasonably clear, the grease ice all behind us, and our earlier annoyance towards Slava dissipated, helped by the good dinner and some of our remaining beers. An impromptu music session followed in honour of our guests – Mike on fiddle, Paddy, Rory and Gary on vocals and guitar and yours truly on harmonica. Henk gave his unrecognisable interpretation of some U2 classics and everyone joined in a very raucous chorus. The Arctic never witnessed a more incongruous concert!

I visited the deck at 03.00 and was alarmed to find that thick new ice had formed all around. Even the toilet had frozen! Slava, who was also up, was very agitated! All hands got a rude awakening and, after a quick coffee, a frenzy of activity got us underway. At full revs the engine was barely able to

Both crews aboard Campina, *secured to an ice floe, as we wait for a cargo ship to collect* Campina.

move us at 1 knot, as we ploughed a furrow through the soft ice. We broke out of the new ice after a mile or so into better conditions – areas of grease ice interspersed with drifting floes. Later in the morning pancake ice started to form. The prospect of overwintering in the ice did not appeal to any of us.

It was definitely time to be out of there!

Rory continues:

We had been towing Campina *all day. In the morning, our progress was painfully slow – almost imperceptible – as we struggled to make 2 knots slushing through the semi-frozen seas. The thin layer of ice was about 2-inches thick, and while normally this would present no problem, it was a different story when towing a larger boat than ours, with her steering jammed. Mick and Kevin went aboard* Campina *and Mick backed the foresail to act as a counter to the jammed rudder. It worked somewhat and while the boat could not sail in a straight line, the wild veering from side to side had lessened.*

We made our way slowly to the rendezvous point and decided to moor onto one of the larger 'grounded' icebergs. We used separate mooring lines from Northabout *and* Campina, *for added security.*

Then it was time to wait.

About five hours later we noticed a very strong beam of light in the northern sky. It was like a spotlight advertising a nightclub. Gradually, the beam came down from the sky, until eventually, the rescue vessel Archenesky *appeared on the horizon and the beam turned out to be its searchlight.*

I personally was very happy with this practical demonstration of the curvature of the earth, and I now had no doubt that the earth is round!

It was about another three hours until the rescue ship reached the agreed rendezvous point and it was now 3am. The wind had strengthened to a force 5 and the temperature had dropped to about minus 100 degrees Celsius. As we prepared to deliver Campina *to its rescuer, we dressed in our warmest clothes.*

As I went over the bow of Northabout *to retrieve the ice anchors, the thought crossed my mind that I really should be wearing crampons! After my feet slipped on the sea-washed iceberg the first time, I also had the thought that I should have a rope around my waist! Unfortunately, I had neither.*

I released Campina's *ice anchor first. Of course, it was the one that was furthest away, and as I made my way across the iceberg to retrieve it in semi-darkness, I felt the shake of the berg as it was hit by another passing berg. The seas were now throwing ice-cold water over the berg and it was not a great place to be. With the ice pick giving me some grip, I made my way on my knees to the ice anchor and dug it out. I threw it towards* Campina, *and they hauled it in.*

Now only Northabout's *ice anchor remained. I moved steadily, but the shaking of the iceberg had increased and it was with a sick feeling in my stomach that I realised our berg was actually breaking up! I felt like a cartoon character, and just hoped that I would end up on the right part. I dug out* Northabout's *anchor and rather than throw it, I carried it back towards the boat – if anything was going to happen, at least I could hold on to it!*

A few minutes later, I was back on board – shaken, but not stirred!

In darkness, the 30,000-ton freighter *Archenesky* had arrived and anchored 400 metres off, showing great skill in positioning the ship at an angle to the wind, to give us a lee.

With all lines recovered, we motored towards the ship, the strong wind making it difficult to control our tow. To further complicate matters, a floe drifted in between *Northabout* and *Campina*. With luck and some tricky manoeuvring we managed to clear the floe and *Campina* was positioned under the ship's crane and secured to their awaiting lines. Once *Campina* was secure we lost no time in getting away from our very hazardous position. Our mast was in great danger of getting entangled in the ship's gear and lifeboats. Very soon, in a remarkable display of cargo handling, *Campina*, with mast stepped, was craned aboard *Archenesky*. Quickly their anchor was raised, and without any delay they were bound for Tiksi, with Henk returning to his previous overwintering base.

The navigation season for small craft was now well and truly over. Cape Chelyuskin had proved to be an impassable obstacle in 2004. We now reverted to our fall-back plans of overwintering in the river port of Khatanga, 300 miles south.

Archenesky later delivered *Campina* to Murmansk where repairs were carried out. Henk overcame further difficulties on the Norwegian coast and arrived home to the Netherlands.

Henk has now given up his dream to sail the North East Passage.

To Khatanga and Overwintering

With the departure of *Campina,* we again considered our options. It was obvious the ice-breaker *Vaigach* felt we would be damaged by the heavy ice at Cape Chelyuskin. And having seen how quickly the sea was freezing, and the damage that *Campina* had sustained, we decided not to risk *Northabout* any further.

Khatanga in Siberia, showing cranes uploading ships delivering coal. The entire area is covered with 10 metres of flood-water in winter.

Top: *There was a lot of interest in our voyage in Khatanga and Colm is seen here being interviewed by the regional television news crew.* Right: *The English teacher invited our musicians to play Irish tunes in the classroom. Left to right: Paddy on bodhrán, Michael on fiddle, Gary on guitar and the watchful teacher behind.*

Slava indicated we would find all facilities in Khatanga, including an airport, which would make it a good place to lay-up for the winter. This seemed like the only suitable place. We certainly did not want to return all the way back through the ice to Tiksi. Khatanga, a riverside town, lay 150 miles up the Khatanga river, a total distance of 300 miles from where we were.

After a long sail up the estuary, we entered the river proper in the morning.

The only problem was that we didn't have charts of the river. At the estuary mouth, the river was wide and deep so we were able to enter with caution.

Slava got on the radio and shortly afterwards we saw the pilot boat approaching. Instead of coming gently alongside as all pilot boats do, this one struck us a glancing blow amidships, damaging the toe rail and sweeping away the guard rail stanchions. On board were a group of men arguing and shouting. They passed us a book of charts and nearly rammed us again in the process. To our relief they went away.

The river meanders all over the place, though well marked with buoys and transit towers. In width, the river was about equal to the Shannon estuary, with low-lying ground on each bank. There were sandbars and islands and constant course changes, a great test of old-fashioned navigation.

By evening we were overtaken by a small ferry, the *Taymyr*, newly built, on its maiden voyage to take up duty in Khatanga as a river ferry. We followed closely behind; as they were familiar with the river, we were able to let them do the navigating.

As night approached, the *Taymyr* and *Northabout* anchored. Both boats were away at first light, though the morning was foggy.

Soon the tundra changed colour from its usual brown to a yellow/green as the inland climate mellowed, allowing stunted Siberian larch trees to grow on the riverbanks.

By 10.00 we saw the smoke of the power station of Khatanga and as we turned the final corner the town became visible. There were a couple of ships unloading at the 'dock' and we were pleased to see two floating cranes at work. The arrival of the new ferry was a big event for the locality. All the townspeople turned out to see her and she was welcomed with the town sirens wailing and the ships' hooters blaring. We too were an attraction for the locals; we were the first yacht ever to visit Khatanga. Colm was interviewed and featured on the local television station. Slava disappeared into town with an old friend, a ship's captain.

Khatanga is an old town; a plaque on a public building proclaimed its 365th anniversary. Mining is the main industry now that the military are gone. The indigenous Dolgan population and the later Russian settlers seemed vibrant to us compared to those in the newer Stalinist Russian towns we had previously visited. Khatanga is now the base camp for many North Pole expeditions.

We played and sang in the restaurant and school, met interesting people and their families, visited their homes, and walked on the tundra.

Our priority now was to get *Northabout* lifted out and secured ashore. This proved to be easier said than done. What seemed to us like a simple crane lift from the water to the shore was deemed impossible. Eventually, the problem was explained; the water level rises 10 metres with the spring melt water. The storage area on the beach, which we planned to use, would be completely underwater. There was no truck large enough in Khatanga to transport *Northbout* to a secure location. Slava's friend offered us a solution; he could hire us a river barge in which we could store our vessel for the winter. It would be safe from thieves and vandals – he would guarantee security. The word Mafia was mentioned with a grin. For this service he wanted a mere $12,000!

We were caught; he held all the aces and he knew it. Slava did not help our negotiations when he mentioned that *Campina* had paid $30,000 for his sea-lift. We mentioned going back to Tiksi rather than pay his price. Eventually we did succeed in negotiating the price to a more acceptable but still very high price. Then we waited and waited. Our bags were packed but we could not book our flights until *Northabout* was secured. We again waited all day on Sunday, and then, without warning, it all happened. A tug appeared with a barge, another tug towed *Northabout* to the crane, the mast was un-stepped, and the giant crane placed *Northabout* in the hold of the barge. The hatch covers were replaced and tack-welded in place. Never was *Northabout* so secure!

On Tuesday 14 September we boarded a flight for Moscow, and after another flight via Paris, we arrived in Dublin the same day.

On the flight home, we made our plans to complete

Top: Northabout *being lifted from the water.* Above: Northabout *in the barge hold for the winter.*

the journey next year. If that proved impossible, we would have to investigate the possibility of shipping *Northabout* home as deck cargo on an ice-strengthened ship.

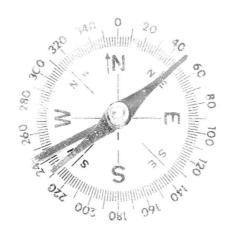

17

DISASTROUS VOYAGES
IN SIBERIA

The North East Passage has had its share of marine disasters. Amongst some of the better-known voyages are: Captain Robert Bartlett on the *Karluk;* Valerian Albanov on the *St Anne*; and George Washington DeLong on the *Jeannette*.

The three voyages all have a common problem: poor organisation and poor leadership.

The Doomed Voyage of the Karluk

Karluk, under the command of Captain Bob Bartlett left Victoria, British Colombia, Canada, in 1913, bound towards the Canadian Arctic on Stefansson's voyage of discovery. Bartlett was one of the most experienced Arctic captains; amongst his previous exploits he had sailed with Peary in his attempts to reach the North Pole.

This Canadian expedition's goals were to map and discover new lands in the Arctic and map part of the unknown Canadian mainland. The *Karluk* was joined by two schooners, *Alaska* and *Mary Sachs*, at Nome, Alaska, which were purchased to handle the additional men and supplies

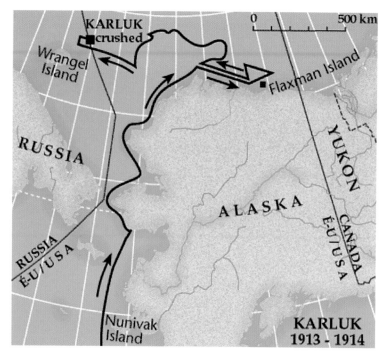

The drift of the Karluk.

needed, as the scope of the expedition was expanded. Though the expedition was funded by the Canadian government, it was badly organised from the start. The Norwegian explorer, Roald Amundsen, described Stefansson as 'the greatest humbug alive'. As the expedition's ships sailed near Barrow off the Alaska coast, the *Karluk* became beset in ice. It drifted first along the Alaskan coast then northwards and westwards. Stefansson and five crew members left the *Karluk* and dog sledged to the Alaskan shore, abandoning the *Karluk* to its fate. The two smaller schooners were able to navigate the shallow water as far as Collinson Point, Alaska, where they were forced to overwinter.

Soon after Stefannson's departure, a gale drove *Karluk* westwards with the ice. In the hurry to leave Nome, the supplies were not properly stowed. Their winter clothing was stored aboard one of the other ships. The three ships had planned to meet at their winter base on Herschel Island and divide the supplies between the ships.

The *Karluk*, still beset in ice, drifted helplessly towards the Bering Straits, then towards Siberia.

After drifting for months, land was eventually sighted again, believed to be Herald Island. Four of the crew attempted to walk to the island and were never seen alive again. Eleven years later their bones were found in their campsite on Herald Island. They left no clue as to the reasons for their demise – a large stock of tinned food and a rifle were found nearby.

The *Karluk*, meanwhile, continued to drift and was squeezed by pressure ice and finally sank in January 1914. Showing leadership and courage, Captain Robert Bartlett rallied the crew and succeeded in reaching Wrangel Island (Ostrov Vrangelya) on 12 March, after the most gruelling journey across the ice ever recorded.

Conditions on Wrangel Island were horrific – three men died. Food was scarce, quarrelling developed and the survivors divided into two separate camps.

Realising that there was little hope of surviving for long on the inhospitable shores of Wrangel Island, Captain Bartlett and Kakaktovik, his Inupiat hunter, crossed the treacherous ice to the Russian mainland to organise a rescue attempt. Having reached the mainland, their troubles were far from over. They were still 400 miles from the nearest town where help might be found. After a long march across Siberia's frozen wastes, with some assistance from the local hunters, they reached Providenia in the Bering Strait. There they had the good fortune to meet with the American whaler, *Herman*, which took them to Alaska. In Alaska, Bartlett was able to arrange for the rescue of the survivors on Wrangel Island.

Jennifer Niven vividly describes the horrors they endured in *The Ice Master*.

Saint Anna: The Epic Survival Story of Valerian Albanov

By a strange coincidence, 1914 was the year of three remarkable sea epic rescues.

While the *Karluk* disaster was being played out in the Arctic, Shackleton lost the *Endurance* in Antarctica and made his epic small boat escape journey from Elephant Island to South Georgia.

At the same time, and at the other end of the world, a lesser-known drama was also taking place. The *St Anna's* crew were struggling to survive in Siberia.

The Russian ship, *Saint Anna*, set out in 1912 from Archangelsk under the command of Georgi Brusilov with plans to find new whaling grounds and sail the North East Passage. The crew comprised 22 men and one woman, a nurse. Brusilov may have been influenced by Nordenskiold's (incorrect) suggestion that the Kara Sea was ice free in late summer. *Saint Anna* was under supplied and had an incompetent captain. At least that's how Valerian Albanov, in his book *In the Land of White Death*, describes it. Albanov was chief navigation officer and former second in command. In the Kara Sea, 'the ice cellar', the *Saint Anna* became beset in an ice field off the Yamel Peninsula. At that stage some of the crew walked across the ice to the shore where they saw the tracks of reindeer herders, who could have offered salvation. For some reason they elected to stay with the ship. Albanov was relieved of his command by his captain, for reasons that have not been explained. For a year and a half, the *Saint Anna* drifted north with the ice. Eventually, with no sign of the ice breaking up, Albanov and thirteen companions, with the captain's permission, left the ship and attempted to walk the 235 miles to Franz Joseph Land. They built improvised sledges, kayaks and skis; they set out marching south on the drifting ice. For every six miles they walked, the ice carried them back two miles, a gain of only four miles. Albanov proved himself to be a truly strong-willed man; he had to threaten his slacking companions with his revolver – to urge them onwards.

Facing starvation, sub-zero temperatures and the loss of most of the team, Albanov persisted. He and Konrad, his last surviving companion, finally made it to Cape Flora, the same cape from which Fridtjof Nansen was rescued twenty years earlier. Their trek across the ice had taken an appalling 90 days. By a miracle they were rescued eleven days later by the *Saint Foka*, a supply ship looking for Sedov, a missing Russian polar explorer. Aboard *Saint Foka*, which was leaking badly, they succeeded in reaching Russia, only to be caught in the first skirmishes of the First World War, a conflict about which they knew nothing.

The *Saint Anna* or its crew were never seen again. Albanov and his companion Konrad were the only survivors.

The Loss of the US Expedition Ship, *Jeannette*

The US *Jeannette* expedition under the command of George Washington DeLong left San Francisco, California, in July 1879, with the object of sailing to the North Pole, through what was then believed to be open water beyond the Arctic ice pack.

The *Jeannette* was a naval expedition, though financed by the newspaper magnate James Gordon Bennett. Bennett had bought the British steam bark *Pandora* and renamed her *Jeannette*. She was rebuilt by the navy and strengthened for a drift in the icepack. Despite the costly re-build, the *Jeannette* did not have the strength required for polar exploration.

DeLong and a navy crew sailed for the Bering straits in July 1879. In addition to the navy crew a number of civilian specialists were also on board. Amongst them was Jerome Collins, an Irish engineer from Cork. Collins was employed by Bennett as a reporter and meteorologist, and immediately found himself in conflict with DeLong.

DeLong was a strict disciplinarian and a martinet. As a civilian, Collins felt he wasn't under navy regulations, employed by and reporting only to Bennett. In fact, he actually was forced to sign on as a seaman. For not taking exercise on the ice, because he was engaged in scientific work, Collins was arrested. He was not the only crewmember to be arrested by the authoritarian DeLong.

DeLong planned on reaching Wrangel Island before 'going into winter quarters'. They entered the ice in early September, and drifted in its grip until June 1881, when she was broken up by the ice and sank.

DeLong led his men, dragging three boats, on a journey lasting nearly three months, across the hummocked ice to the ice edge. They launched the boats and reached the New Siberian Islands after a harrowing time in the ice-strewn sea.

DeLong may have been a poor leader but he now showed his dogged determination.

As they set out for mainland Russia a storm blew up separating the boats. One boat, under the command of Lieutenant Chipp, was lost with its crew of eight men and never seen again. The other two boats reached the coast at the Lena Delta, though at widely different points. One of them, with eleven men led by George Melville, had the good fortune to land at the delta's south-east corner and soon found the main stream. They met with the local Tungus who provided them with food and shelter. Melville decided to walk inland to Balun, a settlement from where he might find help from Russian officials to organise a search for the other missing boats. But first he rested his men, an understandable decision considering the ordeal they had come through. For this delay he was later severely criticised.

Melville had proved himself an extremely resourceful engineer during his time aboard the *Jeannette*. His ability to keep the machinery running in extremely difficult circumstances, and his skill in adapting the generator motor to drive the ship's pump, are a testament to his ability.

DeLong's boat, with his thirteen men, were not so lucky. They came ashore in a maze of muddy streams elsewhere on the delta. They struggled through the newly-formed ice as they waded through the marshy ground, and were soon exhausted. Amazingly, Collins was not allowed to assist as he was still under arrest! And despite their weak condition DeLong refused to abandon his records. From there on DeLong's journal is a pitiful record of the deaths of his men. DeLong sent two of the strongest men forward to try to meet with locals for assistance. Near starvation, they finally met locals but were unable to make them understand that their colleagues were dying nearby. They were taken south. Luckily, a message they had written found its way to Melville. He immediately joined them in Bulun and, finding out where DeLong's camp was, set out to find him. By 11 November he was in the vicinity of DeLong's camp, as he found the cached expedition records. He was running out of food and abandoned the search as he was now convinced DeLong was dead. Many unanswered questions surround the decision to abandon the search.

The wreck of the Jeanette *on 12 June 1881.*

The search was resumed the next spring in 1882, and the bodies of DeLong's party were found. They were taken back to New York and from there, Jerome Collins' body was shipped to Ireland, to be buried in Cork. His funeral has been called 'The longest funeral in the world'. A naval enquiry was established to enquire into the tragedy and the mistreatment on board the *Jeannette* of Jerome J. Collins. This enquiry was regarded by many as a 'cover-up'. It failed to reveal the true facts. DeLong had many influential friends.

In the museum in Tiksi we saw DeLong's heartbreaking written accounts of the expedition's last days and the cross that marked their resting place.

As *Northabout* sailed past the Lena Delta in 2004, we cast a wreath on the waters in memory of our countryman and the others who died so tragically.

Wreckage from the *Jeannette* was found many years later on ice floes off the west coast of Greenland, inspiring Nansen, the Norwegian scientist and explorer, to attempt to reach the North Pole by deliberately setting *Fram*, his ice-strengthened ship, into the ice pack off Siberia. Nansen drifted in the *Fram* for a year and reached 84 degrees north before setting out on skis on his unsuccessful attempt to reach the pole.

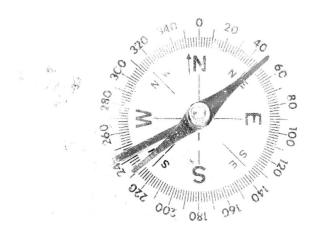

18

KHATANGA

June 2005

How quickly the winter passed! It seemed such a short time ago that *Northabout* was laid up in a river barge in Khatanga and now Tom Moran and I were on our way back.

The wintertime back home had been taken up with fundraising activities. We felt fortunate and grateful to get the financial support of Volvo Cars Ireland Ltd, Permanent TSB Bank and Dromoland Castle Hotel. In addition we had again raised funds with the proceeds from slide shows we had presented at various locations and with donations from our well-wishing friends.

One must admire the spirit of the people who live in the riverside town of Khatanga. Their life is a perpetual struggle for survival against the elements and the harsh winter.

The winter snow cover is a blessing in a way, as it hides the junk abandoned everywhere. The outskirts of town are littered with abandoned military hardware, trucks, tanks, tracked vehicles, machinery of all kinds and rusting barrels. Further out of town are the rusting remains of huge dish antennae, built to track US missiles. The 'industrial estate' lay in ruins, the various enterprises long

Abandoned military hardware is a common sight in Siberia; this troop carrier is on the main road in Khatanga.

since failed. Tom remarked that the only business that would thrive here would be a scrap metal yard – there was certainly no shortage of raw material for such an enterprise.

There are no roads to the interior; the River Khatanga and its tributaries extends many hundreds of miles inland and it is the only link to the interior the Khatangese people have, apart from air services. During the short summer, supplies of coal, oil and fuel for the power-generating station are delivered from the eastern seaports by convoys of ice- strengthened ships led by an ice-breaker. Smaller river-going vessels trans-ship the supplies upstream to isolated communities. In winter the temperature drops below minus 50 degrees, freezing the river solid, enabling tracked vehicles to use the river as a highway. The hinterland is mainly tundra and frozen lakes, and as one travels further upstream, gradually the tundra gives way to the *taiga*. *Taiga* is the Russian name for this forest that covers much of the sub-Arctic, where stunted Siberian larch trees grow in the boggy ground.

This same untamed river is also the cause of many of Khatanga's problems.

In the spring and summer thaw, the river water starts to flow under the ice initially. Then, as the ice starts to break up, huge chunks of ice start to move downstream.

Soon all the melt water is moving, carrying the ice. The ice gets jammed at restrictions causing a build-up of water and ice behind the dam. Soon the pressure of water and ice breaks the dam and a cascade of water-borne ice rushes downstream, sweeping away everything in its path. At Khatanga the water level rises by 10 metres and any floating dock structures are swept away by the wall of ice.

An e-mail from our friend Vladimir, who was keeping an eye on ice conditions in Khatanga, announced that the river was nearly ice free and that the barge would soon be wanted for river service. In sunny Mayo this was the call Tom and I were waiting for. We quickly arranged flights and arrived in Khatanga on 12 June 2005, to launch and prepare *Northabout* for sea. The sea ice would not break up until mid August but in the meantime we needed to make sure everything was in order on board. There was a long list of work to be done. Because of the previous year's hard driving through the sea ice, the overworked gearbox was leaking oil again and in need of an overhaul. And Tom was the man to do it, having done the same job in Oregon.

Getting to Khatanga was an ordeal in itself. There were no direct flights to Khatanga at that time of year. Our route from Moscow, crossing three time zones, was via Krasnoyarsk and Norilsk. In Norilsk we had 'big problem' with border guards. We were taken off the plane and into an office in the basement of the airport building, where a high-ranking official interviewed us. He insisted we should not be there, Norilsk being a restricted area. After an hour of questioning in an intimidating room underground, we got the all clear following many phone calls to Moscow. Two armed guards put us on a plane bound for Khatanga.

The plane was full; all the passengers were in good form having spent the waiting time drinking vodka. Plane travel in Siberia was not burdened with safety precautions. The exit doors were blocked with loose baggage, the flight attendants took their seats on the baggage and without any further delays we were airborne.

Natasha and Vladimir looked after Northabout *during the winter.*

The Khatanga Hotel.

In Khatanga the border guards were waiting for us, and once again we were taken away and questioned. Eventually, after going through the same rigmarole as before, we were welcomed to Russia. Vladimir was waiting for us and took us to the hotel. The town was recovering from the severe winter freeze up; the winter temperature had dropped to minus 57 degrees. Pipe welders and plumbers were working everywhere, replacing frost-damaged heating and plumbing pipes.

After the long flight and delays we were irritable and exhausted and looking forward to a shower and a good night's sleep. It was not to be. There was no water in the hotel, not even in the toilets, and when we spoke to the receptionist we got a tirade of abuse. At least that's what it sounded like to us, judging by the agitated tone. We soon fell asleep though, despite the noise of people partying in the adjoining rooms.

In the morning, a visit to the harbour brought more surprises. The harbour was unrecognisable from last year, the wide foreshore area was no longer visible and was now under 10 metres of melt water. The river, which was so placid last year, was in full spate carrying the last of the river ice downstream at 5 knots.

More importantly there was no sign of our barge! We learned that Valodia, the barge owner was out of town, and nobody knew for how long. With the help of Vladimir and the harbour master, we were assured of assistance in the morning – 'maybe' – a phrase we were to hear many times over the next two weeks.

To our relief, we saw our barge on our second day. It was towed in by harbour tug from its winter mooring and anchored in midstream. The tug crew brought us out for a look, the hatch covers were removed and all seemed well. There was a dangerous chop on the river, caused by the strong northerly wind against the 5-knot river current. The tug crew promised to bring us out to start our work the following morning.

Next day, we got to work. With much trepidation I switched on the batteries, pushed the engine pre-heater button for ten seconds and pressed the starter. The engine started immediately. I breathed again. The on-board min/max thermometer which was stored in the chart storage drawer had recorded an inside winter temperature of an amazingly low minus 37 degrees.

The frost had damaged the calorifier (hot water tank) which we had overlooked in our winterising work. Colm's champagne bottles had also succumbed to the frost. The glass was in bits. Colm had made provision for a celebration for our anticipated rounding of Cape Chelyuskin. The champagne could be easily replaced, and indeed we were now learning to survive without hot water showers.

We replaced the depth sounder transducer which had been damaged last year with a new unit, and spent the next days completing the items on our list of work to be done.

No matter how often we enquired at the harbour master's office about getting a crane lift to launch, we could not get any more satisfactory answer than 'maybe tomorrow'. Neither Tom nor I could speak Russian, which made communication very difficult. Vladimir, with his basic English, was a great help; without his assistance we would have been in serious difficulties. The time to our return flight was rapidly running out which added to the pressure on us. The uncertainty about a launch date meant that Tom couldn't remove the gearbox. To do so was to risk was being launched with the work half-done and finding *Northabout* afloat but immobile, just as our plane was about to take off. As we waited, we made an inventory of the food on board, and to our great delight, Tom found another stash of cheese lost under Paddy's bunk, now matured but in perfect condition.

We were constantly surprised during our attempts at shopping in Khatanga and indeed throughout Siberia. Nothing outside a Siberian building reveals what can be found inside. The shops don't exhibit their wares, nor can you pick up your own purchases; the assistants hand them to you. Very few shops have display windows, or indeed anything to indicate that a shop exists. Of course, the locals know precisely where to shop.

Daily we had discussions with the harbourmaster about launching; there was always a 'big problem' – one day it was too busy, next day it would be loading coal, next day loading oil, then,

After waiting nearly two weeks, finally Northabout *was launched from its winter storage barge by the floating crane in the background*

'no contract'. Now we discovered that before we could be launched, we had to sign contracts for the crane lift and also an agreement for mooring in the harbour, both very officious-looking documents. With contracts duly signed, we again waited, and waited. Days went by as we continued our work in preparing *Northabout*. Then, on our ninth day in Khatanga, just as we were about to give up hope, the floating crane appeared with a full crew, and in no time the crane slings were on *Northabout*, and she was launched. Stepping the mast was difficult in the windy conditions, with such an unwieldy crane. Nevertheless, the mast was rigged in less than an hour with the loss only of the masthead VHF antenna.

We bade farewell to the crane crew and motored closer to the beach to a slightly more sheltered area and anchored. What a relief to have a proper living area again, good bunks, cooking facilities and a toilet that worked!

Tom checked out the machinery in our last days in Khatanga and declared *Northabout* ready for sea. The gearbox overhaul could wait until later, providing we regularly checked the oil level. With a certain amount of relief we boarded the plane for home, Tom vowing that he would never complain about anything ever again after his experience of life in Khatanga!

With arrangements made with Vladimir and his father to provide 24-hour security, we left *Northabout* on anchor and boarded the plane for the long journey home.

The Jarkov Mammoth

In Khatanga the locals say that it was the mammoth that put their town on the map.

In autumn 1997 a local Dolgan boy, Kostan Jarkov, spotted a large tusk protruding from the tundra near Khatanga.

Around this time, a Frenchman, Bernard Buigues, was operating a tourist Arctic business, Cerpolex, taking tours to the North Pole from Khatanga. Bernard heard about the find and immediately took an interest. He delayed his return to Paris in October of that year in order to have a closer look. With a hair dryer he began to melt an area around the permafrost and found hair attached to skin and, of course, the two large tusks.

He returned the following year with ground-penetrating radar and discovered a completely intact adult mammoth. This was a rare find.

There was huge interest in the find and over the following two years, he and his team excavated a massive 23-ton block of permafrost containing the mammoth and transported it by a heavy-lift helicopter into a cave specially cut into the permafrost under Khatanga.   ▶

Top: *The mammoth men.* Above: *Bernard telling us about finding the mammoth.*

We were given a tour of the frozen laboratory by Bernard, who painstakingly works on the collection of hundreds of tusks and bones on these extinct animals.

At the end of the cave, in a separate chamber, there was the frozen block containing the Jarkov mammoth. Two 9-foot long tusks weighing 100 lbs each protruded from the block. We got to see and feel the skin and hair of this mighty creature that died about 23,000 years ago.

At the end of the Ice Age, the denuded marshes and loose sand became a death trap for these huge animals, which stood nine feet high at the shoulder.

By the early twentieth century the remains of 50,000 mammoths have been taken from Siberia. The last known woolly mammoth to have roamed the earth was in Wrangel Island a mere 3,700 years ago.

We hope the Jarkov mammoth will indeed bring prosperity to Khatanga.

Michael Brogan

Mammoth tusk collection in the ice cave at Khatanga.

19

KHATANGA
TO CHELYUSKIN

The Siberian winter was a cold one – a real Russian winter. The ice pilots say that's a good sign. They say cold winters are followed by warm summers and that's what we need for the north-flowing Russian rivers to discharge warm water to melt the sea ice.

Colm in Moscow, together with Alexei, our Russian partner, had been beavering away constantly chasing our permit, and yet it was only at the last minute – five minutes before closing time in fact – that I finally collected the document from the offices of the Murmansk Shipping Company in Moscow, at 17.55 on Friday 5 August. What a relief to have the permit in my hands at last! Initially, we had thought that it would be viewed as an extension of last year's permit but that would have been too easy and too logical. Instead we had to go through the same procedure as before and began at the beginning, re-submitting all documentation again.

Having got the permit we were able to relax for the weekend before going to Moscow's airport for the long flight to Khatanga.

Before we left Dublin we had a serious setback to our plans. As our check-in time at the airport was at 04.30, to save time in the morning we loaded our bags into Paddy's car the previous night,

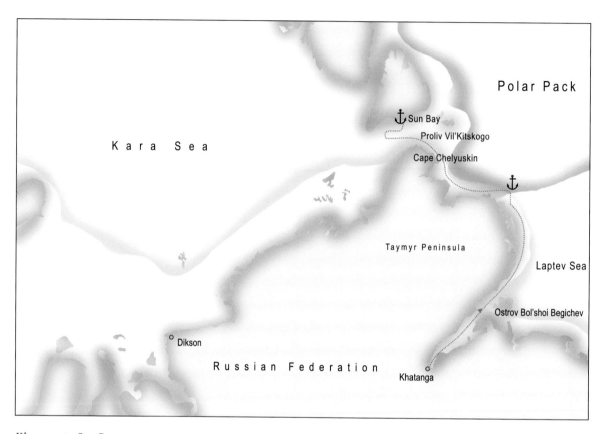

Khatanga to Sun Bay.

and – yes, you have guessed it, the car was broken into. We didn't discover our loss until we were at the airport and saw our ransacked bags. I won't mention anything about the words that were spoken at the sight!

This was a very serious loss. Apart from our cameras and personal items, we lost two laptop computers and the satellite phone. The laptops were loaded with our digital charts and other information, which was essential to our voyage.

Never ones to be beaten by a setback like that, we organised plan B as soon as we arrived in Moscow. We bought a new satellite phone and a laptop. The satellite phone was a mandatory requirement for the ice pilot to keep his twice-daily call to Murmansk. Thanks to the wonders of modern technology, Brendan had a backup of all the information at home, which he transferred to our new laptop via a fast e-mail connection to Rory at a Moscow internet café. The transfer time took seven hours, despite the fast connection! This saved the day. Where would we be without the expertise of Brendan and Rory and their two days' work? The mind boggles at the wonders of modern technology.

We met our ice pilot Slava, who had again been assigned to us for this year's voyage. The crew was complete. We flew to Khatanga and checked into the airport hotel. The hotel was still without water!

We brought *Northabout* in from her anchorage to a berth alongside some rusty sheet piles. Paddy and I chose to vacate the hotel in favour of the comforts of the boat.

Over the next few days we loaded our supplies on board and filled up with diesel. We filled the water tank directly from the river, it being cleaner than the town's piped supply. The wind from the north continued to blow hard. We had to wait until we got a more favourable wind.

In the port a river tanker was loading oil and a cargo ship was unloading coal onto the beach.

Again this year, *Northabout* had to be surveyed before we could leave Khatanga. Slava completed the survey with the assistance of the harbour master's surveyor, and for this service we were charged a cash fee of $300.

The river water level started to rise; overnight it had risen by a foot and continued to rise daily. Soon our berth became untenable as the sheet piling disappeared under the water and we moved and tied up at the ferry berth.

The stockpile of coal on the beach was soon surrounded by water and unloading had to stop as the river continued to rise.

We Irishmen were treated to some unaccustomed sights. What at first appeared to us as drifting trees in the river, on closer inspection turned out to be the antlers of herds of caribou swimming across the river on their annual migration. Each group of about twelve were led by a stag, swimming

Northabout is moored alongside the 'dock' while uploading coal for the power station continues.

furiously across the fast-flowing river. To get a closer look, we motored out into the river and got some photographs as they swam alongside us. As soon as they reached shore, they all ran up the river bank and disappeared across the tundra.

Reindeer are similar to caribou though slightly smaller. They were domesticated in northern Eurasia about 2,000 years ago. Today, they are herded by many Arctic peoples in Europe and Asia including the Sami in Scandinavia and the Nenets, Chukchi, Dolgan and others in Russia. These people depend on the reindeer for almost everything in their economy including food, clothing and shelter.

Clockwise from top left: *Overnight the river level started to rise and the coal supply was soon surrounded by water; the fuel tanker has to drive into the water to deliver fuel to the ferry; migrating caribou swim across the River Khatanga.*

Herds of migrating caribou were constantly swimming across the river.

Leaving Khatanga

It sounds like the words of a song but there was nothing to sing about in Khatanga!

The ice reports were discouraging. A tanker coming from Tiksi with an ice-breaker escort reported very slow progress through the ice. The thought of spending another winter in Siberia was worrying. Once again we could do nothing but wait for a favourable south-westerly wind to clear the ice away from the Taymyr Peninsula.

In Khatanga harbour, a cargo ship, the *Toliati*, lay at anchor awaiting the ice break up like ourselves. She damaged her propeller shaft getting there last year and had to overwinter while repairs were carried out. She was now returning to Murmansk. The trip to Khatanga was an expensive one for her owners, with only one cargo delivered in two seasons. We decided to make our way down river and wait in the estuary for the ice to break up.

We were privileged to meet Khatanga's Russian Orthodox Priest, who suggested a blessing of the boat and crew before departure. This ceremony duly took place on board, with quite a long prayer reading and sprinkling of holy water. We were presented with icons of Saint Nicholas, the patron saint of sailors, and a small folding triptych of sacred images.

Slava said his prayers each morning before the holy images with great sincerity. It made me remember how as children in Catholic Ireland we had the temerity to pray for the conversion of

The Russian Orthodox priest wished us well and blessed Northabout *and its crew before we left Khatanga.*

Russia. We were led to believe that all Russians were atheistic communists; we knew nothing about the ancient Russian Orthodox faith.

On Thursday 18 August, fortified with the blessing, we set sail down the Khatanga river, with farewell sirens and ships' hooters blaring. Some no doubt were sorry to see us go, since our contribution to the town's economy was significant.

The navigation down river was interesting. The river has many sandbanks and islands but the course is well marked with buoys and transit lines. The 24-hour daylight helped too, as did the three-knot current. By Saturday morning we were out of the river and making our way north between Bol'shoy Begichev Island and the mainland, with occasional ice floating in the sea. We met the tanker bringing Khatanga's annual oil supply, several days overdue because of the heavy ice encountered. They told us of heavy ice outside the shelter of the island.

By mid afternoon we were at latitude 75 degrees, 50 minutes north, only a few miles short of last year's 'furthest north' so hard attained then. As the day progressed the ice became more dense but we continued to make some progress.

Slava, on his regular link-up with Mr Babich, the controller of shipping in Murmansk, informed us that there was heavy ice inshore and advised us to move offshore to where the ice-breakers operate. Reluctantly, and with misgivings, we took his advice. Our experience so far had indicated that a shallow-draft vessel like ours can find leads close inshore. And our misgivings proved right; by midnight we were stopped by solid 10/10 polar pack ice.

We were now faced with the same dilemma as last year when we had anchored at Martha Island for eleven tedious days, unable to advance and surrounded by ice. Should we wait or attempt to go backwards? We took a third option; we radioed the ice-breaker on patrol in the area, the *Sovietsky Soyuz*, a second-generation nuclear-powered vessel.

The conversation that followed was polite. They had never heard of us and had no instructions to assist us. Slava tried his charm but to no avail. When charm won't work, the old military strategy must be used; outrank them! He phoned Mr Babich in Murmansk and had a long conversation.

The ice filled in around us as we waited in silence, not knowing what might happen. Then at midnight we got the word we wanted to hear – the ice-breaker was on its way, travelling at 18 knots through the ice.

Out of the fog, at 3am it broke through, and completed a circle around us. Last year we had been impressed at the size of the *Vaigach*, but this monster, the *Sovietsky Soyuz*, was astounding in size, 148 metres long and displacing 23,000 tonnes. Powered by two 171-megawatt nuclear reactors, transmitting 75,000-horse power to its propellers, it can break ice 2 metres thick. The ice churned up by its propellers was frightening to see – gigantic blocks of ice were being bounced around. Were we going to be sunk by our liberators? Then, as the ice-breaker stopped, everything settled down. The *Sovietsky Soyuz* led the way and we followed in her wake, in a clear path 50 metres wide. The path was kept open by the latest device to be fitted to ice-breakers; a series of air-jets all along her sides, which blow the broken ice clear. In this marine highway we followed for four hours, travelling at 7 knots. At 07.30 we were out into the Laptev Sea and in clear water. *Soyuz* hove to and we exchanged presents and bade goodbye. We got on our way towards Cape Chelyuskin, the Cape Horn of the north, now only 110 miles away.

A light snow fell at times. The weather was cold and foggy but we didn't care; we were in high spirits. Our goal was in sight. After Cape Chelyuskin the ice reports indicated the sea was virtually ice free. The sea was flat calm, with a few loose floes.

The nuclear ice-breaker Sovietsky Soyuz, *77,000 horse power, arrived to clear a path through the ice for the 90 horsepower* Northabout.

Top: *Rory and Jarlath in a snow shower.* Above: *The team celebrate leaving the landmark Cape Chelyuskin astern. Back row, left to right: Rory, Michael, Slava, Jarlath and Colm; front row, left to right: Kevin, Paddy and Gary.*

On Monday morning at 08.00 22 August Cape Chelyuskin was abeam, the temperature was minus 2 degrees, ice cover 1/10, and the sea flat calm.

Cape Chelyuskin, the most northerly point of mainland Russia, was unremarkable low-lying ground, unlike the mountainous southern capes, Cape Horn or the Cape of Good Hope.

A tot of Midleton Irish whiskey was served to celebrate the rounding of this landmark.

Soon we encountered pack ice again, on our port side. We skirted it to the north for a while but gradually we were surrounded by ice floes once more. Then more bad news came our way – a call from Mr Babich advised of a changing situation. Northerly gale force winds were forecast which would move the polar pack ice down on us. He advised us to run for shelter; he recalled as a young seaman sheltering from a gale in Sun Bay (Solnechnaya) on Bolshevik Island, and recommended we shelter there. This meant backtracking 20 miles through heavy ice floes, and it was not going to be easy. But clearly there was no choice. To stay out in the forecast gale would mean we could be crushed between floes, or be driven ashore on Cape Chelyuskin.

So we set our course to Sun Bay, tackling each floe one by one. For a time we made good progress and then we entered a band of nearly solid pack ice. From the masthead Paddy could see clear water about one mile further on. Knowing there was clear water ahead we tackled the ice with renewed vigour. We rammed, we pushed, we poled, we backed up and tried again; never did we abuse *Northabout* so much. The centreboard and the rudder took a hammering; I wondered would the structure survive the punishment. The engine too, was pushed to its limit, as were the crew. But eventually we succeeded at last in breaking through the ice and shortly after midnight we dropped the anchor in placid Sun Bay.

What a day! From our first early morning encounter with the ice-breaker, motoring in freezing snow, to rounding

Paddy, from his perch on the cross-trees, has the good news that there is clear water a mile ahead.

Above: *Dramatic, menacing sunset at the appropriately named Sun Bay in the New Siberian Islands.* Right: *Nearly through the ice barrier and into the safety of Sun Bay; pushing floes aside with poles.*

Chelyuskin, to again nearly being trapped in ice, and now safely at anchor in a bay at our furthest north, 78 degrees, 12 minutes. After a meal we all collapsed into our bunks, exhausted from the long, strenuous day.

After midnight, the sunset produced the strangest red colour in the sky; at these latitudes there was no darkness. The entire sky became an angry orangey red hue. Was this the sailors' warning?

The gale arrived during the night. We lay snug at anchor, while outside the ice piled up and the snow fell. The stormy weather raged for four days, as we thanked our lucky stars and Mr Babich for our secure anchorage.

Ashore we saw new bear paw prints in the snow; they led down to the shore and back. The bear, unbeknown to us, had swum out for a look at our boat during the night. As there were no paw marks on deck we assume he didn't attempt to come on board.

On the east side of the bay were the ruins of a Russian polar station. It was abandoned because of the numerous fatalities from bear attacks. During a lull in the weather a group of our crew went ashore in the dinghy for a look around the barren landscape. There was little to be seen ashore and a bear attack was uppermost in their minds, so they wasted little time in sightseeing. In the event of a bear attack, we had better protection as we now had a gun acquired by devious means. Don't ask how, or where – a veil of secrecy protects the guilty.

The gales had brought ice down from the polar pack and now a 100-mile band of ice blocked our way, where last week there was none. Outside our bay the *Toliati* was also at anchor awaiting better conditions.

On our fifth day in Sun Bay the weather improved. We raised anchor to cross the bay to look at the polar station and we had just anchored again when we got a radio call to get ready to join a convoy heading west.

Paddy Barry gives us a brief history of the North East Passage:

Bolshevik Island is midway along this 3,000-mile north coast of Asia. We are at 78 degrees and so are on a convenient platform to view it. Indigenous people have lived here and travelled its shores from time immemorial, 'before the white man came'.

White men came north for the fur. The eastern boundary of the tzars' empire extended to the Pacific Ocean and indeed into northern America. Its western lands into Europe were well known. To the far north, the map was largely blank.

Tzar Peter the Great, in 1725, resolved to amend this. His Great Northern Expedition, over the next twenty years, 1,000 men in five detachments, achieved remarkable results. Their methodology was to travel eastward on known inland routes. Meeting the big north-flowing rivers, they would build boats and sail to the Arctic shores, mapping east and west. The names of their leaders adorn the map, Bering, Deznev, Laptev and our own current favourite, Semion Chelyuskin, who in May 1742 reached Asia's most northerly point by sledge. For four successive summers he tried and failed to sail round it.

Further expeditions over the next 100 years filled in added detail, led by men like Billings, Litke and Wrangel, all involving overwintering and help from native Chukchi, Yakuts, Dolgan and Nenets.

In parallel, commercial endeavour brought the Russian Pomors, coastal traders, eastward from the White Sea and into the lower reaches of the Kara Sea.

The British traders Chancellor and Willoughby followed them in 1553, reaching Moscow upriver and overland.

Dutchman Willem Barents, trying in 1597 to reach Cathay through a North East Passage, reached the northern coast of Novaya Zemlya, New Land. He and his men overwintered there, unintentionally. The foundations of his hut remain.

The first to traverse the North East Passage was the wealthy and well-travelled Swedish Baron Nils Nordenskiold. He, in his 300-ton Vega, *made it from west to east in 1878 and was beset only a short 100 miles north of the Bering Strait. He got through the following summer.*

Norwegian Fridtjof Nansen traversed much of the passage eastwards as far as the New Siberian Islands in 1893, before deliberately setting his Vega *into the ice for a northern two-year drift.*

In 1899 these Arctic seas saw an icebreaker for the first time, the Yermak.

In 1914-15 the ice-breakers Taymyr *and* Vaigach *journeyed from Vladivostok to Arkhangelsk, the first Russian transit.*

They discovered the islands at which we are now anchored, the Northern Siberian Islands. Their leader, Boris Vilkitskiy, took the losing side in the 1917 revolution but nonetheless his name was given to the strait between Bolshevik Island and Cape Chelyuskin.

The Soviets closed Russia to foreigners but before this became effective, Roald Amundsen, he of the North West Passage and the South Pole, made a west to east transit in Maud *between 1918 and 1921.*

Russian ice-breakers have since made the transit, the nuclear ones virtually at will.

However, this is infrequent as the needs are supplied from the east by their Far East Shipping Company and from the west by their Murmansk Shipping Company.

Small boat passages of note have since been:

Yakutia	*1991-1993*
Apostle Andrew *(Nicola Latau)*	*east to west, 1998-99*
Sibir *(Sergei Cherbakov)*	*west to east, 2000-2002*
Vagabond *(Eric Brossier)*	*west to east, 2002*
Dagmar Aaen *(Arved Fuchs)*	*west to east, 2002*

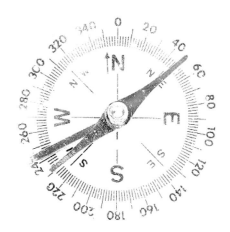

20

CAPE CHELYUSKIN
TO DIKSON

I wrote this on Friday evening, 26 August:

'The gales of the past four days have abated, the sun is now shining brightly; the temperature, despite the sunshine, is minus 2 degrees, and we are impatient to be on our way. We are leaving Sun Bay at last, to join a convoy. Mr Babich has instructed us to proceed to a position N77° 59′ E102°38′ where we will meet our old friends the ice-breaker *Vaigach* and the cargo ship *Toliati*.'

When we joined the convoy we were surprised to find that we were being led in an easterly direction and we could only assume that the reason for heading in that direction was to skirt some ice. And so it was, but we also met with the ice-breaker *Sovietsky Soyuz*, which was going our way too. Soon afterwards, we all turned westwards, *Vaigach* leading the way and breaking the ice, followed by *Sovietsky Soyuz*, with her side jets blowing the ice clear, then *Toliati*, and finally *Northabout*, the last in line.

We rounded Cape Chelyuskin three hours later, our second time in five days, this time in heavy ice, motoring along in style at 7 knots, in the ice-free path behind the convoy.

All Saturday we continued to make good progress. In the afternoon we saw a mother bear and

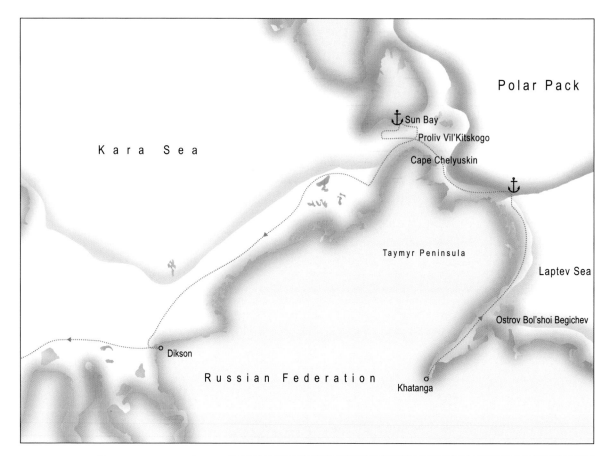

Above: *Sun Bay to Dikson.*
Right: *The storm of the past week has blown polar ice down on Cape Chelyuskin and it is now impassable without ice-breaker assistance.*

three cubs on an ice floe. Mother bear led the cubs and hid them behind a chunk of ice. Their white coats made them virtually invisible against the ice-floe background. So well did the bears blend into the icy scene that without the giveaway three black spots of their snouts and eyes, and the slightly yellowish tint of their fur, we would have passed them by unseen. In Greenland we were told that the polar bear covers his snout with snow when stalking seals to complete his camouflage.

At midnight we broke out of the ice and sailed in the clear waters of the Kara Sea. *Sovietsky Soyuz* and *Vaigach* departed with sirens and hooters blaring and we waved our good friends farewell.

A mother bear with cubs is barely visible on the ice floes.

The ice-breakers were returning to Cape Chelyuskin to escort another convoy around the icy cape. Without the dedication of the ice-breaker fleet, it would be impossible to supply the northern Siberian towns with their annual requirements of food, coal and oil.

Sunday started out cold, warming as the day went by to plus 3 degrees. Visibility was mainly poor, becoming foggy at night. By midnight Dikson was less than 60 miles away. By 10 o'clock next day, on a dull and foggy morning, we secured alongside at Dikson Docks.

We were met at the docks by a contingent of border guards and officials and, rather unusually, by a group of women who were interested in our yacht, the first they had ever seen. After the usual posturing by the border guards, we were welcomed to Dikson. One look around the docks with its dereliction and decay spurred us into action to re-fuel and leave as quickly as possible. There was little sign of shipping activity in the harbour.

Dikson is on an island near the mouth of the Yenisei River and was named by the explorer Nordenskiold after one of his sponsors, Oskar Dickson. Later this name was Russian-ised to Dikson. We were told the population is about 1,000 people. The winter lasts for ten months and even in summer the weather is never pleasant.

Clockwise from top: *Convoy; Dikson docks; going for a shower in the power station admiring a custom-made tundra trike.*

We succeeded in having water and diesel delivered without delay but getting food took a lot more time. Despite it being only ten days since our last shower, we felt we should make the effort to get clean and so we arranged a visit to the Dikson *banya* – the sauna. The *banya* was a modest affair in the power station, sensibly using the waste heat.

The *banya* is a wonderful experience, starting with a normal shower, then into the sauna, taking one's place on the lower tiers of the seating and moving upwards as one becomes accustomed to the heat. Beating oneself with leafy branches and taking cold showers, the time passes easily. We observed that some Russians were discussing important contracts and drinking cold beers. Apparently this is where the business deals are done, in the absence of a golf course. Clean and refreshed at last and, as it was now evening, we decided to have a meal ashore and leave in the morning. The meal was a good one and developed into a music session in the restaurant – so good, in fact, that it was 11.00 next day before we departed for Murmansk.

21

DIKSON TO MURMANSK

We left Dikson on Tuesday 30 August in very poor visibility; the foggy conditions persisted, so we never got a look at the delights of the town. From the little we saw through the fog, there didn't appear to be any highlights.

Since our skirmish with the ice as we approached Sun Bay a vibration was noticeable when motoring, which I assumed was caused by a damaged propeller blade. We had two spare propellers on board but were reluctant to change them in the freezing water. To replace a propeller underwater in warm water is a tricky operation; dive down, remove the locking split pin, remove the nut, fit the propeller puller, tighten the puller, remove the old propeller; fit the new propeller, replace the nut and split pin and don't drop anything! Everything is much more difficult in freezing water. Just imagine trying to hold a small nut underwater without dropping it. We decided to leave the changeover of propellers for the moment. By keeping the engine revs below 1500 RPM the vibration was minimised and our speed could be maintained at 6.5 knots. Hopefully we could get a quick lift-out in Murmansk to change props.

But a new challenge was in the offing; the long-range weather forecast indicated a gale was on

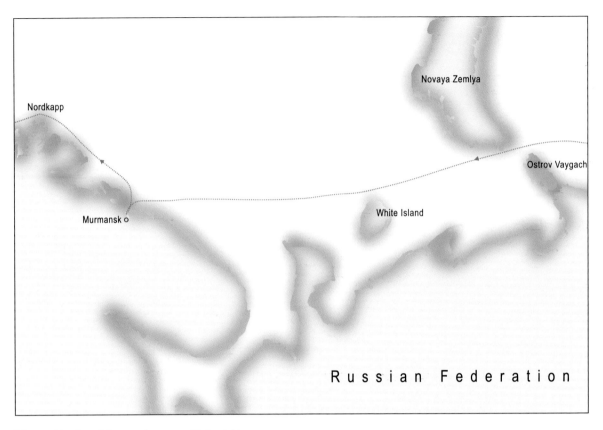

Novaya Zemla to Murmansk: our goal is in sight.

the way; we hoisted all sail to keep up speed, hoping to arrive in Murmansk before it hit.

Our route towards Murmansk took us by White Island and through the 'Iron Gate' south of Novaya Zemlya (the big island). The temperature had now increased to a more comfortable 6 to 8 degrees. We had finally left the ice behind us, to the crews relief. There would be no further threat from polar bears. So as we had no Russian firearms licence, we dropped our gun overboard.

After Rory and I started our watch at midnight, we were thrilled to see a magnificent display of the aurora borealis, the 'northern lights', in the northern sky. We called all the crew to come and have a look. This was no ordinary display – it was out of this world: shimmering curtains of pale green, white, blue and yellow. All were enthralled and stayed up while the display lasted. Our normally uninteresting watch turned into a pleasant couple of hours.

Kevin Cronin describes the Aurora.

Night sky viewing has been disappointing so far. A combination of long Arctic days and fog have allowed us only an occasional glimpse of the moon and none of the stars. Now that we are at lower latitude and the nights are getting longer and darker, we expect to do much better.

We are treated to a magnificent display of the Northern Lights (Aurora Borealis).

Last night we were rewarded for our long wait. It was a clear night; only the thinnest sliver of moon sitting on the horizon and real darkness setting in after a glorious sunset. All the stars, planets and constellations we are familiar with slowly flooded into view. At about 1 am the Aurora started its display. Jarlath and Rory were on watch with Mike and myself below having just finished ours. They shouted down to us to come up and look. Quickly we were all on deck.

And it was spectacular!

A white trail arched across the sky from west to east over the top of our mast and sail. It was shimmying and shivering like a curtain in a breeze. Other patterns formed. Streaks of light, white brush-strokes lightly daubed in groups on a steel-blue sky, circles and whorls and undulations of all shapes. And within each pattern a wild pulsing and vibrating. The dominant colour was white but at the fringes there were flashes of red and greens. It was mesmerising.

We watched for over an hour as the great celestial artist wielded his brush and stroked the sky with wraith-like patterns and curtains of light.

We tried to photograph it but it proved difficult to do so from a moving boat. Later Gary captured a few images when we were ashore in Norway.

Definitely the highlight of my voyage!

It was in this area that the *Saint Anna* was beset in the pack ice in 1912, the beginning of its fatal drift to the north, which culminated in its eventual sinking.

In the morning we anchored near the lighthouse on White Island and had a quick run ashore for a walk on the tundra. There was little to be seen, apart from a magnificent beach, endless tundra and a nuclear-powered lighthouse. The nuclear 'power pack' was a remarkably small unit.

On Friday afternoon the mountains of the island of Novaya Zemlya were visible to the north. The Dutch explorer, Willem Barents, was forced to winter on its northeastern shore when his ship

A nuclear-powered lighthouse on White Island.

was trapped in the ice in 1596. The crew built a house ashore using timbers from their ship. Most of the crew survived and later escaped in two open boats. Sadly, Barents himself was not so lucky; he died in one of the boats.

It was on Novaya Zemlya that the Soviet Union's nuclear weapons were tested, killing 10,000 polar bears in the process (and possibly many humans too, nobody knows). Here, in the past, nuclear waste was dumped in the sea, doubtlessly still causing nuclear contamination. And if that wasn't enough, the pilot book warns of mines in the area, another reason to keep well clear.

Saturday brought force 6 southwesterly winds and choppy conditions. We plugged onwards through the bumpy seas, keeping up our speed, trying with all our might to get in ahead of the gale.

On Monday morning Rory and I finished our watch and handed over to Paddy and Colm. Our course was set between Kil'Din Island and the mainland, just outside Murmansk fjord. We were having a nightcap when suddenly armed men in survival suits boarded us. They approached without warning from astern in a RIB. These were lively lads – it was amazing to see how quickly they leaped on board with Kalashnikov assault rifles at the ready.

After much shouting from them, Colm determined that they were the coastguard and that we should have stopped and checked with them before proceeding. After checking our documents, they relaxed a little and instructed us to return the way we came, a distance of two miles, to their mother ship. We tied alongside their ship, while they made phone calls to Moscow. After six hours we got the all clear to proceed to Murmansk. During that time all our documentation and permits were scrutinised and passports were checked, again and again. The off-watch coastguards relaxed

Apprehended by the coastguard. 'Why didn't you stop?'

in our saloon and over coffee and breakfast we became the best of friends; they brought vodka on board and really made themselves at home. With some difficulty we finally persuaded them to leave – one has to show respect to men with Kalashnikovs.

Having been cleared by these coastguards, we were told it wouldn't be necessary to go through the clearance process again in Murmansk. They would telephone their friends and tell them what fine fellows we were – that they had checked us through.

With joy in our hearts we motored the 30 miles up Murmansk fjord, and waited as instructed for the pilot boat, which eventually appeared and guided us to a floating jetty. Soon it was blowing hard from the south. We just made it into shelter ahead of the gale. Then the border guards appeared, and unbelievably we found we had to go through the same entry procedure all over again. Our clearance at sea counted for nothing with these men. The Iron Curtain is gone, but the 'paper curtain' still flourishes and thrives. Clearance took over four hours; every document was checked again and again. They finally relaxed and welcomed us to Murmansk and asked that we give them twenty minutes notice prior to our departure. We were then free to explore the town. We looked forward to going ashore and celebrating, for this was the completion of the North East Passage, our goal for the past two seasons.

Top: *The off-duty coastguards relaxed and celebrated our success in completing the North East Passage.* Above: *Entering Murmansk Harbour; on the hill above the city is the remarkable statue to the unknown soldier, known as Alosha.*

Murmansk, with a population of about 400,000, is the largest city north of the Arctic Circle, and is ice free all year. During the Second World War it was heavily bombed because of its role as the destination of the Arctic Convoys bringing supplies to the Allies from across the Atlantic. For its resistance it was designated a 'hero city', a title awarded by the Soviet Union to twelve cities for outstanding heroism.

The size of the town was impressive; it was modern and businesslike. In the shipyards and dry docks, work was underway on all kinds of vessels. Mile-long trains were hauling ore and coal on the rail tracks by the docks. This was a completely different Russia to that which we had seen previously in other Siberian towns.

We treated ourselves to hotel rooms and got cleaned up for a night on the town. We ended up in the Irish bar, where Paddy was given centre stage, singing rebel songs. In the euphoria his guitar was lost – we suspected it was borrowed by a couple of dodgy-looking characters in black leather jackets.

In the morning we called on the Murmansk Shipping Company and met the controller of shipping, Mr Babich, to give him our thanks for his assistance with ice-breakers. We expected a huge control room with charts and models of ships in their current positions on the route. Not so. Nicolay Babich had all the information in his head. He was a grand man and modest. He was a big man in every sense of the word; a man of the sea. He joined us for dinner that night. In Paddy's toast to him, he described him as 'a direct descendant of our heroes – the 1740 explorer Semion Chelyuskin, and the 1914 navigator Valorian Albanov, who sailed from this very same Murmansk Harbour – we were honoured (said Paddy) to be in his company.' Nicolay responded with kind words on our achievement on completing the Northern Sea Route. Next day, after farewells, Slava and Colm departed for Moscow, Slava electing to take the train. Rory and Gary took the plane to Moscow on the first stage of their flights home to catch up with work.

We refuelled and replenished our food and water, and planned to leave next day. The propeller change couldn't be arranged and would have to wait till Norway. Though there were repair facilities on offer, it proved too difficult to get work done in the time available in Murmansk.

That night Paddy's guitar was retrieved, on payment of a ransom! A late-night caller to the hotel offered to 'help'. He knew where it might be and would try to get it, for a small inducement in dollars. It was nice to have it returned; it had survived many great voyages, even a shipwreck. After the loss of his hooker, *St Patrick*, the guitar had been washed ashore virtually undamaged in Glandore Bay.

Departure didn't go any better than arrival. We advised the border guards of our intended departure as requested. The officials started to arrive, a customs man, an immigration official, five border guards, a man from port control, a marine surveyor and a port pilot. We had two 'big problems': first, we needed clearance from Moscow, which would take another day at least, and secondly, we couldn't depart from the jetty at which we lay. The port official turned out to be very helpful; he took over, ordered all officials off the boat and instructed us to move to the designated departure berth, a mere 100 metres away! Even for this short trip it was necessary to take on the port pilot.

191

Top: The North East Passage completed, Kevin can finally enjoy that cigar he had been looking forward to for two years. Below: Paddy enjoys his cigar with a drop of whiskey.

Then our new friend, the port official, dealt first with the immigration official; this man needed five copies of the crew details and was surprised we didn't have a photocopier on board. So we laboriously copied out our crew lists for each of the five officials. Next in their turn this port official dealt with border guards, customs and other officials from previously unheard of departments. He overruled all suggestions that we should wait another day and insisted we be cleared. The one item of equipment that impressed everybody was our *Northabout* stamp. Obviously stamped documents carry a lot of weight in Russia. The marine surveyor did a thorough safety survey; the only item, which caused a concern, was our EPIRB (Emergency Positioning Indicating Radio Beacon), which was slightly out of date. He was satisfied when I signed an affidavit that it would be serviced when we got to Norway.

After all documents were duly completed and stamped, we were allowed to go. Even though it was now 22.00 hours, dark, and raining heavily, we got underway, with the port pilot on board. The poor man had no rain wear with him, being used to big ships, but he took it all in his stride, wearing one of our spare waterproofs.

He left us at midnight, when we rendezvoused with the pilot boat. Our instructions were to proceed well out to sea before changing our course towards Norway.

We had a choice of routes for the journey home, the more exposed northern route over the top of Norway or the more interesting route through the White Sea Canal (the Belamorekanal) to St Petersburg and the Baltic. We all agreed we had enough of Russian officialdom and abandoned our plans of transitting the White Sea Canal.

The thoughts of being stopped by bureaucrats at every canal lock was more than we could face. Much as we would have liked to see St Petersburg, we opted for the hazards of Norway's North Cape instead. In retrospect, had we known the delays and difficulties we would face on Norway's coast, the White Sea Canal may have been the easier option but at the time we couldn't have known that.

Russia is a big country, as is the spirit of its people. They have gone through a difficult time since the fall of communism and the devaluation of the Rouble.

The Russian people we met were the finest one could meet anywhere. Their generosity, their pride, their good humour and their warm spirit will always be remembered by all of us. We were never asked for a bribe or inducement, nor were there any suggestions that 'presents' would help smooth the way. We did, of course, pay for services rendered and gave presents to people who helped us.

Officialdom is a major problem; one has to be patient, and be prepared to wait without becoming annoyed or upset. Most officials will try to help but they are tied by their system, which to Western eyes appears unnecessarily complex.

The biggest unforeseen expense was the cost of storing *Northabout* overwinter in Khatanga. The barge owner, Valodia, saw his opportunity, recognising our weak position. In any country, including our own, there are always people ready to take advantage of a situation when they hold all the aces. But looking back on it now, he did get us out of a problem, one that we didn't fully understand at the time. He proved to be a man of his word; he stored *Northabout* securely for the winter and didn't look for any additional payment afterwards.

The border guards caused us quite a bit of trouble, mainly because we, as tourists, were a new experience for them and they didn't quite know how to deal with us, never having dealt with foreigners before. But they were polite, and less aggressive than the Homeland Security Guards we dealt with in America.

Russia is in a state of flux, finding it hard to shake off the old ways. We found there was a reluctance to answer a simple question directly. The most common answer to a question was 'maybe'. Many

Farewell to ice.

officials were reluctant to make a decision. Most decisions were referred to a central authority in Moscow. Maybe their reluctance to make a decision stems from hearing stories from their fathers and grandfathers who were sent to the Gulags for speaking out. Gradually, with Glasnost (openness) and Perestroika (restructuring), Russian society will improve – they deserve better. My great regret was not being able to speak Russian; there was so much I missed by not being able to communicate directly with the people we met. My views on Russia are somewhat limited by the fact that we only saw the Siberian towns and villages – these, I'm sure, don't represent the real Russia.

At 17.00 next day (8 September) we left Russian waters and entered Norway's welcoming territory.

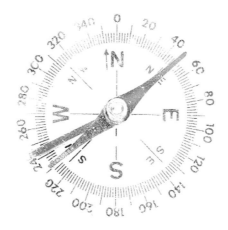

22

NORWAY

As we entered Norwegian waters we contacted Vardo Radio and reported our position and destination. 'You are very welcome to Norway; you may sail on, no problem, please report to customs when you arrive in Tromso.' What a contrast to the way we were greeted everywhere in Russia.

Having seen the whaling stations that the Norwegians had built on the remote island of South Georgia, I had often wondered what drove the men of the north to the south Atlantic to live and work in so harsh an environment. The answer was revealed as we sailed into Norway. Their home environment prepared them well – all the coastal communities lived on isolated islands and they were no strangers to isolation, hard work and self-sufficiency.

We had arranged to meet our new crew in Tromso, Norway, 400 miles distant from Murmansk. Tom Moran, Eoin McAllister and Brendan Minish were joining us for the final leg, having given us a good start on the beginning of the North East Passage from Prince Rupert to Russia.

Shortly after passing North Cape, the most northerly point of Norway, our new computer purchased in Moscow crashed. We had by now become so accustomed to the ease of digital navigation that the loss initially seemed like a disaster.

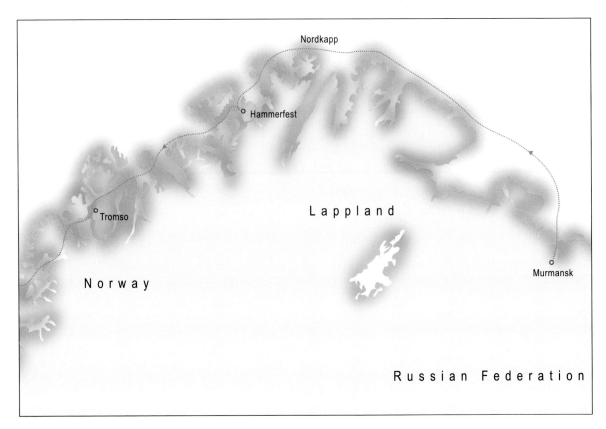

Murmansk to Tromso.

So it was back to the parallel rules, paper charts and dividers. In fact, once we got used to the old technology, it was quite enjoyable again. The only problem was that we didn't have detailed charts of Norway; we had to make do with our large-scale charts.

Luckily, Gary succeeded in hooking up our number two computer to the GPS and we were soon back in the world of digital navigation again.

We sailed the inside passage between the islands and the mainland, passing brightly-lit villages. The contrast to Russia was overwhelming. What wonderful scenery: high snow-capped mountains, deep fjords and colourful houses. Navigation was a pleasure; every rock and headland had a navigation light. The North Sea oil money had been put to good use. The villages all had good newly-built harbours and ferries served the island communities. Mobile phone service was available everywhere and wind power provided electricity to many of these islands.

A westerly gale forced us to anchor for a night to shelter from the severe gusts of cold wind blowing seaward from the mountainous coast, known to sailors as williwaws. As our crew were waiting for us in Tromso, we pushed on in the morning as soon as the gale began to ease.

We arrived in Tromso on Monday morning, 12 September, and were delighted to see our new crew waiting to take our lines on the visitors' berth at the marina.

Top: *Magnificent Norwegian mountain scenery near the Lofoten Islands.* Above: *Most of Norway's population live on the coast.*

Soon we had cleared customs. Tom came aboard and cooked us a full Irish breakfast, for he had brought the ingredients from home. It was election day in Norway and there was much celebrating that night, in which we joined with gusto. We had a meal ashore and our musicians played to a celebrating electorate in the bar afterwards.

We were shocked at the high price of beer, at €7 a bottle. Nevertheless, those high prices didn't put a stop to our celebrations.

Our crew settled in quickly. We enjoyed hearing all the news from home and reading the latest newspapers.

Brendan and Eoin, both IT men, quickly diagnosed the computer problem. The legitimate copy of Windows XP software, which we had installed in Moscow, should have been registered within one month but nobody mentioned this to us, so naturally we hadn't done it. Brendan made the necessary phone call and our computer was back in action. The 'evil man' is how Bill Gates was described aboard *Northabout*, as his attempt to control customers worldwide puts seamen at risk.

In the nineteenth century, Tromso was known as the Paris of the north because its wealthy inhabitants were cultured, well-educated and more fashion-conscious than would be expected for a city 400 kilometres north of the Arctic Circle.

Today the city has a population of over 60,000, and still deserves the title, with its university, theatre, art galleries and museums.

In Tromso's polar museum, Paddy is in the 'crow's nest' with an Arctic fox in the background.

Rainbow on the Norwegian mountains.

The highlight of our visit to Tromso was the polar museum, one of the best to be seen anywhere. In addition to the usual museum pieces on life in the early days, the Norwegian explorers, Nansen and Amundsen, are honoured, with many artefacts from their voyages, including artefacts recovered from Willem Barents' hut on Novaya Zemyla, where the explorer had spent the winter of 1597. Amundsen's telegram announcing his conquest of the South Pole is also on display. A visit is highly recommended.

Our plan now was to sail the inner passage to the Lofoten Islands, then take the sea crossing to the Shetland Islands and from there sail directly to our home port – Westport, a total distance of 1,300 miles. At our normal speed of 150 miles per day we should be home in about nine days. With luck we should be home by 22 September.

With some trepidation, we departed at midday on 13 September into the rain and blustery conditions that were an ever-present feature of wonderful Norway during our time there. That evening we tied up alongside the jetty in Finnsnes for a short break. We were away again at 01.00 in dark, wintery conditions, sailing down the inshore route. For a time the wind increased to 35 knots as we made our way down the narrow winding channel. The waters generally were sheltered, the islands giving protection from the worst effects of the gales. Snow covered the hills down to the 100-metre contour. The temperature was generally in the region of plus 4 degrees.

Clockwise from top: Rorvik; The picturesque town of Rorvik where we were storm bound for four days; the coastal shipping route is well charted and marked with beacons and lights; Rorvik marina.

We entered the beautiful fishing harbour of Svolvar in the Lofoten Islands in the evening sunlight. The harbour is surrounded by high snow-capped mountains and is one of Norway's most picturesque towns. But we could only enjoy the scenery for a short time; we had a long way to go and with some reluctance we left a couple of hours later.

Our plan was to head out to sea from there towards Lerwick in the Shetland Islands, a 650-mile sea crossing, and from there we would take the direct route to Ireland.

We hoisted sail and departed at 23.00 in choppy conditions.

The night sailing was grand but wind gradually increased from a southwesterly direction, directly on the nose. We double-reefed the mainsail, furled the genoa and partly furled the staysail. As the wind further increased we took in the third reef in the mainsail. We were sailing close-hauled, with the engine ticking over, and were very hard pressed. We continued on, with the cold seas sweeping over the deck, encouraged by the forecast of a favourable northwesterly wind.

Conditions didn't improve – in fact they deteriorated; soon the wind was blowing a force 9 gale, forcing us to heave-to for a while. Paddy again assured us 'there is no such thing as bad weather, only weaklings with poor oilskins!'.

At 19.00 as we were not making much progress towards our destination, and with no sign of an improvement in the weather, we turned 90 degrees and ran for the inside channels 30 miles away downwind. We anchored in the shelter of Soroya Island after midnight. All were well after a very rough day and the boat stood up well too. Paddy reluctantly conceded that the weather was bad!

We got the stove going again (it wouldn't stay lit in the rough weather), got warmed up, and dined in the relative comfort of the sheltered anchorage.

As the forecast now indicated continuing gales, we changed our plan, and decided to take the inside passage as far south as practical, to somewhere in the region of Bergen, before attempting the crossing of the North Sea.

In the morning we raised anchor and were underway at 06.30 in light rain showers.

Shortly after midday we overtook the Dutch sailing vessel Bøl, a beautiful traditionally rigged Baltic Trader. Like us, they were on the way to Rørvik.

We didn't know it at the time but Rørvik was to be our port of refuge for quite some time. We arrived on Friday 16 September and couldn't leave until Tuesday 20 because a whole series of gales kept us pinned down.

One couldn't, however, be trapped in a more interesting and welcoming place. We got to know quite a number of people. We enjoyed a great dinner aboard Bøl. We attended a play based on a day in the life of Rørvik in 1902. The actors and audience moved through the original buildings, including the schoolhouse, attended a wedding, mingled with fishermen mending their nets and finally walked down to the shore to wave goodbye to the emigrating boy who was off to seek his fortune abroad. Even though we understood little of the dialogue, we all enjoyed the realism of the play, and were moved by the final song, a slow air accompanied by an accordion, which we know as 'The Leaving of Liverpool'.

Rørvik had many highlights; in the cultural centre we saw a wonderful film on two old men living alone on an island, fishing and farming in the old way, just like in Ireland in the 1950s. Michael, our choir singer, got involved in the Rørvik choir and joined their singing. On Sunday evening we were invited to a choral performance in the church, which turned out to be a memorable evening.

We finally got away at 09.00 on a 'normal' wet day, the wind blowing force 5, later increased to force 8. Before leaving we first had to persuade a ten-year-old boy that it wasn't a good idea to

A German gun emplacement from the Second World War which guarded the entrance to Trondheim Fjord.

run away to sea with us. He was a son of one of our new-found friends and was determined to join us; he had his bag packed and was ready to go. After we set sail we had a most uncomfortable day, being thrown about, bashing into seas, until we finally anchored at 23.45. An equeally uncomfortable night followed with anchor dragging and re-setting. Next day was no better; we motored through another day of gales and secured alongside a pontoon at 18.00 in Brekstad in Trondheim Fjord, having made only 24 miles as the crow flies.

The wind kept us pinned down all next day, and we were thankful to be in a comfortable marina berth. We spent the day sightseeing, admiring the magnificent scenery of Trondheim Fjord. We had a tour of an impressive German gun emplacement built into the hills overlooking the fjord. This was a huge affair with three 10-inch barrels, commanding the entrance to Trondheim. Yet interestingly enough it had never fired a shot in action here, though it had seen action in its previous life on a battleship.

Early on Friday 23 September, Kevin, Gary and Michael left to catch the ferry for Trondheim, to get flights home. We were sorry to see them go but they had run out of time and all had pressing business to catch up with.

The morning was flat calm, and *Northabout* was underway at 06.00. We at last had a full day of fair weather. Was our luck going to change for the better? No. By early next morning we were back in the teeth of a gale. We worked our way into the shelter of a tiny harbour on the small island of Orta and anchored. The anchor didn't hold, so in heavy rain we raised anchor and with great difficulty moved to the exposed jetty and got secured. This was not a good position to be in because the gale was banging us onto the jetty and damaging our lifeline stanchions.

In the afternoon the wind eased, the day brightened and we departed at 17.30 to make the short dash to Alesund. By 21.30 we were securely moored alongside the quay wall in the picturesque setting of Alesund Harbour. That night the wind again increased to force 7 to 8 outside. Happily, now snug in the harbour, we celebrated Paddy's birthday holding a party ashore for him. The weather was no better on Sunday but we were happy to be in a good harbour, with opportunities for sight-seeing, and doing maintenance work.

The city was rebuilt in Art Nouveau style architecture, having been destroyed by fire in 1904. Alesund has a population of 40,000 and is one of Norway's most important ports.

Ahead of us lay Stad, a headland notorious for bad weather and rough seas. Conditions are so bad off the headland that the Norwegians are going to drill a two-mile-long tunnel through the mountain to give a safe inside passage. This tunnel will be big enough for cruise ships to transit it and will avoid the dangers of open sea. In the meantime sailors will have to await better weather to round Stad, as we had to do.

On Monday morning the wind had eased sufficiently to have a go. Stad lived up to its reputation: huge seas, strong tides and, of course, the wind increased to force 7 against us. We were in two minds as to whether we should keep going or run back to Alesund for shelter. The seas were tremendous; a large fishing trawler nearby would seem to completely disappear in the depths of the troughs. We chose to keep going even though we were only making 2.5 knots for a long time. At 18.00, after a day-long strug-gle, we finally tied alongside the visitors' pontoon in Maloy. The distance travelled was a mere 25 miles.

The next day was windy and the forecast was poor for the week. We took advantage of this enforced stop to have *Northabout* hauled out at Maloy Vert, a businesslike boatyard, with a travel-lift crane. We changed the propeller and checked the underwater surfaces. Tom removed the gearbox and rebuilt it. Just like that! Pinions, epicyclical-gears, gaskets and bearings were spread all over the table, as the master mechanic got to work. Seeing all the parts opened up made me happy that we didn't attempt this repair in Russia, where getting the simplest spare parts would have been a nightmare. The boatyard was happy to allow us to do our own work and were able to order spare parts from Oslo for us. Delivery was promised in two days and so it was! So good was the service here that we decided if the weather didn't settle soon we would look at the option of leaving *Northabout* in Maloy for the winter. All our work was complete by Saturday morning but we were unable to leave as the wind still blew hard.

The wind eased in the evening to about force 4 so we decided to have a go, and departed at 20.45 in rain showers. With the new propeller and overhauled gearbox we were able to maintain a speed of 7 knots and headed out into the North Sea again, nearly three weeks after our first attempt. At least the open sea crossing distance was now considerably reduced, having worked our way down the Norwegian coast.

Our route now was directly across the North Sea to the Moray firth on Scotland's east coast and through the Caledonian canal, avoiding the notorious and aptly named Cape Wrath on the

Clockwise from top left: *Tom squeezed into the 'engine room' to remove the leaking gearbox; the gearbox is stripped down to its basic components; trawlers in the North Sea attempting to intimidate us and force other trawlers out of their way. An oil drilling platform is visible in the background, right.*

north of Scotland. For the first few days the North Sea lived up to its reputation: the seas were choppy, weather was misty, the wind force 3 westerly. Many oil platforms were visible, sometimes flaring-off gas, creating an eerie glow in the mist. Later as we crossed the fishing banks, we found ourselves in the middle of Norway's fishing fleet. Large fishing trawlers were everywhere, jockeying for position, as they waited for the start of the fishing season. They were acting recklessly as they tried to force other boats out of their way. Several times we were nearly run down by these trawlers, as they blatantly disregarded the rules for the prevention of collisions at sea. At any one time there were at least twelve trawlers in close proximity to us, as they continued to intimidate one another. A Norwegian naval boat was on patrol amongst them, trying unsuccessfully to keep order. We were glad to get away from them before night time. The night passed without incident, as the weather improved.

The following evening we entered the sea-lock of the Caledonian Canal at Inverness.

23

A HISTORY OF
IRISH ARCTIC EXPLORATION
IN BRIEF

FRANK NUGENT

The involvement of Irishmen in Arctic exploration is very considerable and can be linked to the relatively high Irish contribution to the ranks of the British Navy in the period following the Napoleonic War, when Arctic exploration was at its highest intensity. Irish involvement revolved around three main themes: the study of terrestrial magnetism; the exploration by Navy expeditions for a navigable North West Passage to the Pacific from the Atlantic; and the search for Sir John Franklin's lost North West Passage Expedition from 1848 to 1859. Among the Irishmen who made significant contributions were General Sir Edward Sabine, Captain Francis Crozier R.N., Admiral Sir Leopold McClintock, Vice-Admiral Sir Robert Le Mesurier McClure and Vice-Admiral Sir Henry Kellett. Irish involvement with the North East Passage concerns the fate of two Cork men, Jerome Collins and John Cole, members of the American *Jeanette* North Pole expedition sunk off the Siberian coast in 1891 and with the private Arctic expedition of Sir Henry Gore-Booth (father of Countess Markievicz) in his sailing boat *Kara*, who explored through Norwegian waters to Novaya Zemla during the same period.

Irish North West Passage Exploration

The first theme centres on Sir Edward Sabine who was born in Great Britain Street (now Parnell Street), Dublin. He was educated at Marlowe and the Royal Military Academy at Woolwich. He served in Gibraltar and Canada before returning to London in 1816 to devote himself to scientific studies in terrestrial magnetism, astronomy and ornithology. In 1817 Sabine (then aged 29) was a captain in the Royal Artillery. The problem of longitude had been solved by John Harrison's fourth marine chronometer in 1764. An unresolved problem was the need for a general theory which explained magnetic variation and to correlate known magnetic data with geographic locations, with a view to possibly establishing another method to determine longitude. Sabine's first links with the Arctic occurred when he was appointed astronomer to the Arctic expeditions of John Ross in 1818 and later as scientific officer to William Parry in 1819–20; both expeditions were in search of a North West Passage. He made his first pendulum and magnetic experiments in the Arctic and later on the coasts of Africa and America. He went on to superintend the establishment of magnetic observatories in many territories throughout the British Empire and the collection and analysis of the resulting data collected.

Captain Francis Crozier R.N., from Banbridge, County Down, who lost his life on the ill-fated Franklin expedition. (Courtesy Mr James Crozier)

Francis Crozier

Further voyages under the command of Parry in 1821 to 1823 and from 1824 to 1826 introduced Francis Rawdon Crozier from Banbridge, County Down,

Left: *Vice-Admiral Sir Robert Le Mesurier McClure, from Wexford, who was commander of* Investigator *on its search for Franklin. (Courtesy National Portrait Gallery)* Right: *Vice-Admiral Sir Henry Kellett, from Tipperary, who commanded the* Resolute *in the search for the missing Franklin expedition. (Courtesy National Portrait Gallery)*

as midshipman aboard HMS *Fury*. He also became involved in scientific observation and became a great personal friend to James Clark Ross. In a storm HMS *Fury* became wrecked and all her stores were landed on Fury Beach, which played a role in future expeditions. Meanwhile, another explorer, Lieutenant John Franklin, was sent overland by Barrow to complete two complementary expeditions across Canada tracing the Coppermine and Mackenzie Rivers to the Arctic coast. He successfully mapped 1,100 miles of the Canadian Arctic coastline. However, Franklin did not manage to link-up with Parry as Barrow had hoped. But he did find a navigable section of coastal channel, which in time proved to be part of the elusive Passage.

Sabine, meanwhile, was successful in promoting and administering data collection worldwide concerning terrestrial magnetic observation. In 1835 he translated Hansteen's *Magnetism of the Earth* and produced a first chart, showing lines of equal intensity of magnetic force.

The Lost Franklin Expedition

On Ross' return from Antarctica the pressure was on for a last great effort to navigate the North West Passage. The first issue was to appoint a leader; James Clark Ross was favoured but he made it known he was not interested. Sir John Franklin, with the active support of his wife Jane, made a determined claim for the post and was supported by Ross and Parry. Crozier, who was also considered for the post, did not wish to compete against Franklin, who was his friend. Franklin was given overall command, with Crozier second-in-command in charge of HMS *Terror* and James Fitzjames in charge of HMS *Erebus*. It was with great public expectation the Franklin Expedition left England in May 1845 with a crew of 132. *Terror* and *Erebus* were last seen by the crew of a whaling ship in Baffin Bay, off the west coast of Greenland, in July 1845. When no word was received from them after two years away, concern was eventually raised.

(Frank's book – *Seek the Frozen Lands* – gives a comprehensive history of the Irish involvement in polar exploration.)

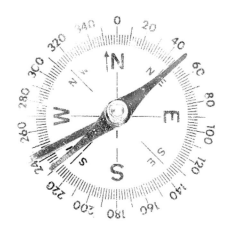

24

THE CALEDONIAN CANAL

It was late evening as we sailed under the spectacular road bridge on the approach to Inverness. The mast passed clear under the bridge deck; even though we had double-checked the clearance, when we looked up it seemed like we would clash. Time was running out as we radioed the canal authorities. The tide was falling fast. The sea locks close two hours before low tide and it seemed like the lock gates might be closed before we got there.

The prospect of spending a night anchored off with the bright lights of the hostelries mocking us on shore was too much to bear, so as any prudent mariner would do, we fired up the engine, and made all speed towards the entrance sea lock. We made it with little time to spare. The lock keeper couldn't be more friendly and helpful. We paid the transit fee, entered the basin and tied up for the night. The transit fee included use of showers and laundry. After showers we were ready to sample the local beer, which seemed incredibly cheap after Norway's exorbitant prices.

Michael Brogan re-joined us in the morning having flown in via Glasgow. John Murray, our filmmaker, was in transit; he would meet us somewhere along the canal and would keep in touch by phone.

Clockwise from top: *The tranquil Caledonian Canal. One-third of the canal is man made, the remainder goes through Lough Ness, Oich and Lochy; an early canal-side suspension bridge; canal locks, one of the 29 on the waterway.*

The majestic Caledonian Canal is 96.6km (60 miles) in length of which 35.4km (22 miles) is man-made. Stretching from Inverness to Fort William, it is one of the great waterways of the world, offering visitors spectacular scenery, amazing wildlife and the world-famous Scottish hospitality.

In the morning we set off refreshed after a good night's sleep and continued up the locks and into the canal proper. Our plan was to get to Fort Augustus by evening, where we had fond memories of good nights' entertainment ashore during previous transits.

The Great Glen divides the Highlands of Scotland with its series of lochs and was therefore considered an ideal site for a canal from as early as 1726.

A series of surveys were carried out throughout the eighteenth century but it was not until 1802 that any action was taken on the proposals.

The Caledonian Canal, as we know it was designed by Thomas Telford, the greatest of Scotland's civil engineers. Funded by the British government and constructed between 1803 and 1822, it was the first state-funded transport undertaking in British history and remains under public ownership to this day.

Though initially intended to provide a safe transport route for naval frigates during the Napoleonic Wars, the Caledonian Canal did not serve a military function until the First World War. Nonetheless, the Canal has played a significant role in the development of the Highland economy, fostering trade between east and west, as well as with Germany, Holland and the Scandinavian countries.

After crossing the scenic Lough Ness, we stopped for the night in Fort Augustus, which is conveniently situated about halfway through the canal. That night was a memorable one. After dining ashore, our musicians performed in both pubs and got a rousing Scottish welcome. Paddy even displaced the resident singer, the famous David Holt, on the bandstand. David took it in good spirits and gave us a CD of his songs.

Ben Nevis, Scotland's highest mountain in evening sunlight, photographed from our canal-side berth; next morning it was covered in snow.

We got underway in the morning, ascended the series of locks to the summit and made our way through Loch Oich and Loch Lochy. We tied up for the night at Fort William, at the top of the staircase lock that descends to the sea lock at Corpach. John Murray arrived by car and spent the day filming our transit of the canal, while we relaxed and enjoyed the spectacular scenery.

The weather forecast for the next few days was poor, low pressure dominating the British Isles. We needed a settled spell for the final stage of our voyage to Westport. The windy conditions prevented us going to sea; it continued blowing hard for four days, while we fretted and fidgeted. On the plus side we now had a snug berth with toilets and showers nearby. Ben Nevis got a covering of snow as the days went by.

As we waited for the gales to pass, we took a sightseeing trip to see Captain Scott's polar ship, the *Discovery*. The vessel is now restored and is afloat as a museum exhibit at Discovery Point in

Captain Scott's wooden polar ship the Discovery, *preserved in Dundee.*

Dundee. She was one of the last wooden three-masted vessels built in Britain. One can marvel at the massive proportions of its timbers, designed to resist the polar pack ice.

We also took a trip to visit Tom Moran's grandfather's grave in Perth; he died in 1942 as a young migrant worker and was buried far away from his native Curraun.

This was a poignant visit for us all; it made us remember the many workers who never came home from Scotland.

We watched the weather forecast carefully. We needed a reasonable 48-hour settled spell and the indications were that after the gale blew itself out on Sunday night we should have an improvement on Monday 10 October.

25

SCOTLAND TO WESTPORT

On Monday 10 October at 08.30 we started the descent down Neptune's Staircase, a remarkable series of locks that took us down to sea level. The weather was still terrible, windy and wet, but the forecast was good; wind easing to force 4-5 south-westerly.

We left the shelter of the sea lock at 11.30 and sailed into a choppy sea. We continued sailing down Loch Linnhe, the high land giving us protection from the worst effects of the seas. After a quick call into Oban for diesel, we continued motorsailing into the dark Monday night. We left the Island of Mull to starboard and Colonsay to port, unseen in the mist.

Despite the bumpy seas, Tom produced an excellent meal of roast Scottish beef, served with potatoes, cabbage and peas. This was one of those 'lifesaver' meals that can revive flagging spirits and it put new life in us all.

Inishtrahull light, on Ireland's north coast, welcomed us to our home waters at 05.00 on Tuesday morning. Our speed was 6.5 knots, not bad in the rough seas and the force 5 south-westerly wind. Visibility improved during the morning; ahead we could see the coast of Donegal, Tory Island and Mount Errigal in the distance. As we sailed through Tory Island sound, a bonfire blazed near the

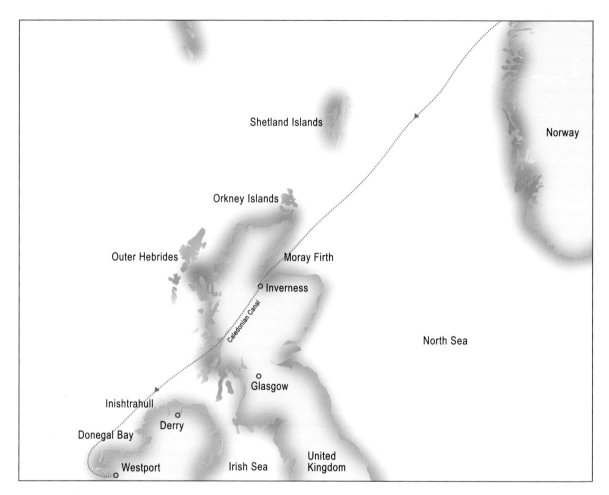

Norway to Westport.

lighthouse, which Michael insisted was lit to welcome us home. Once past Bloody Foreland the crew, in high spirits, enjoyed a pleasant daylight sail across Donegal Bay towards Erris Head.

At midnight, Eagle Island was abeam, with its lighthouse perched high atop the cliffs. Early on Wednesday the lonely Black Rock light was left astern in a heavy swell.

As dawn broke, after we rounded the high cliffs of Achill Head, we were on the home run. We were quite pleased with the passage time on the trip from Scotland; if we deducted the time going into Oban for diesel, we had covered 250 miles in 41 hours, at an average speed of 6 knots; not bad going for the rough sea conditions.

We picked up a visitor's mooring on Clare Island at 06.30 on Wednesday 12 October and tried to grab a few hours sleep.

Four years and four months had elapsed since *Northabout* sailed out past Clare Island in 2001 at the start of its polar journey. Now, as we returned to the island, every one of our crew marvelled at how quickly the time passed!

As Paddy observes on the topic of crew and time:

We were a mixture of old and young. One of the benefits of being old, or at least older, is that fundraising is easier. The bank manager knows you and among your friends are some who can make it possible. The young lads do the heavy hauling and dragging, most of it; in fact when something needs doing everybody jumps to it.

Time flexibility is important. As we've said many times, 'To travel in the Arctic is to wait'. Crew need to have extra time, ideally be open ended. Northabout was never caught because of crew time, although naturally some of our crew had less time than they would have wished.

We generally, on this trip, and on others, have been away for about three months or so at a time. This duration coincides with a number of parameters, the navigation season in the Arctic, maximum time away from home and work, and depth of pocket.

But there is another time feature. I have seen that eight to twelve weeks is the optimum duration for the hard going that Arctic travel entails, while keeping resilient, enthusiastic and congenial. After that duration the physical and mental metabolism slows.

Some fundamental differences remain between part-timers such as us, with shore jobs, and those who make their living as 'expeditioners'.

For those who depend on expeditions for a living, it can become something of the tread-mill, or as Shakespeare observes;

'If all the year were playing holidays, to sport would be as tedious as to work.'

The Circumnavigation Completed. The Wanderer Returns.

Our destination, Westport, now only 14 miles away, couldn't be entered at low tide, so we relaxed for a couple of hours. The morning was beautiful in the quiet island harbour, with clear green water and its spotless white sandy beach. Ashore we were overlooked by Granuaile's castle, the stronghold of the sixteenth-century pirate queen.

There was no rest for us: Chris O'Grady, the island hotel proprietor, arrived and presented us with a bottle of whiskey. Word of our arrival was out, telephone calls from the press and our friends kept us awake. At 10.30 it was time to go. Under full sail we got on our way, with the rising tide. As we made our way across Clew Bay, Gerry Casey, Rory's brother, met us in his helicopter. Through the open helicopter doors, our past crew members Rory and Gary were waving and photographing as the chopper hovered low and close. The familiar Croagh Patrick, Mayo's holy mountain, partly covered in cloud, watched over us. The Achill lifeboat and a flotilla of our sailing friends' boats gave us an escort. The television and press intercepted us in chartered boats, all eager for interviews.

We raised the flags of all the countries we had visited – Greenland, Nunavut, Canada, the USA,

Above: Northabout *sails past Croagh Patrick. Clare island in the background. Right:* Northabout *flying the flags of the countries visited.*

the Russian Federation, Norway and Scotland's flag of Saint Andrew – all fluttering gaily on a masthead halyard.

At 12.30 on Wednesday 12 October, *Northabout* was secured at Westport Quay at the same berth that she left four years previously. Since then she had covered 20,000 miles, many of them in shallow, ice-strewn water.

We left Westport in 2001 planning to do the North West Passage. As time passed, with the North West Passage completed, our ambition grew, culminating in the transit of the North East Passage. *Northabout* dominated our lives for several years from the beginning of building in January 2000 to the completion of the polar circumnavigation in 2005.

People continually ask us, why would we want to sail in such difficult conditions? Was it worth the effort?

We have seen parts of the globe seldom if ever visited by man. We have met with the last of the subsistence hunters of the far north. We have seen amazing wildlife in its natural habitat. We have been scared stiff frozen stiff, and sometimes, bored stiff waiting. We also had some wonderful sailing, and great times ashore. The camaraderie generated among the crew in undertaking such a challenge, and deep unspoken satisfaction at having completed such an arduous voyage, are to me values that are unique and irreplaceable. My answers to those questioners will always be 'yes, it was definitely worth the effort!' The most frequently asked questions are 'how did you get along together? Were there many arguments, and what is your next project?' The answer to the first question is – yes of course, there were some tensions at times, particularly when we were waiting while delayed by ice. The frustration of days slipping by with no progress being made was trying but nothing could be done, only wait and read one's book or play cards. The entire crew was entirely dedicated to our goal and there was never any serious argument. The difficulties we had with Slava were understandable, mainly caused by communication problems and the Russian 'no need to know' attitude. I'm sure Slava felt at times he was sailing with a strange mixture of weird sailors and musicians. The music sessions on board certainly were a great help in relaxing in those times of stress, no doubt helped also with our daily ration of beer! As to our next project, we are not professional adventurers, we are happy to have done what we set out to do and none of us have any plans at the moment for further adventures.

A great crowd of family, friends and well-wishers met us at Westport Quay. The children's band from Westport's *gael scoil* was there to greet us. Our friends from Westport's hostelries provided

Westport Town Council honoured us with a civic reception in the newly refurbished Customs House art gallery.

us with food and drink. The TV and press were genuinely welcoming and we were glad to get an opportunity to publicly thank, through the media, everybody who helped us.

The members of Westport Urban District Council were waiting and honoured us with a civic reception in the newly-restored Customs House art gallery. The rest of the day was spent partying in Westport and reminiscing over the high points of the voyage. It was great to see our family and friends again and to meet in such happy circumstances. Late at night the crew shook hands and parted; the voyage was over but the bond connecting the group will last forever.

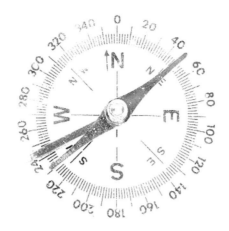

AFTERWORD

The time has come for me to pay tribute to the whole *Northabout* team.

A journey like ours involves work and organisation that only a group of willing, able and congenial people can make possible and enjoyable.

Sailing from Westport to Illulisat with Paddy were: Gearóid Ó Riain, Pat Redmond, Harry Connolly, Eoin Coyle and Cathal De Barra.

The North West Passage team were: Paddy Barry, Jarlath Cunnane, Kevin Cronin, Michael Brogan, Terry Irvine, Gearóid Ó Riain, Frank Nugent and John Murray.

The North East Passage team were; Paddy, Jarlath, Kevin, Michael, Colm Brogan, Gary Finnegan, Rory Casey and Slava Laskevich.

Kevin, Michael, Jarlath and Paddy did both the North West and North East Passages.

Eight of the eighteen played musical instruments, though thankfully not all at the same time but we came pretty close to it at the crew changeover in Anadyr.

From Prince Rupert, to Anadyr, Russia, Jarlath and Paddy, were joined by Eoin McAllister, Joan Burke, Tom Moran and Brendan Minish. For the final run home from Norway, Tom, Eoin and Brendan rejoined us in Tromso.

The crew who sailed the North West and North East Passages. Left to right: Jarlath, Michael, Kevin and Paddy.

In between, as we cruised Alaska and British Columbia, we had many crew changes; we were joined by the following friends at different times; Ben McDonagh, Richard Brown, Michael McGarry, Michael Brown, James Cahill, John Magee, Micheline Egan, Anne Doherty, Michelle Rowley, Verina, Mick Corrigan, Seamus Salmon and Fiona Cunnane.

There were the many friends who helped in the fifteen months of building *Northabout*. There were also those who made financial contributions and, very importantly, others who helped raise funds. There was Brendan and Paul who kept the communications radio base and the website going and finally there were the many friends we made on the way. We thank you all.

We engaged with the local people wherever we went. Most travellers *take* – pictures, information and memories. We tried to *give* a little, mainly through our music – it has a beguiling influence and is an irresistible force in opening communication.

The technical reliability of *Northabout* was fundamental to our success. Isolated areas of the world have no breakdown service. The Arctic is demanding on equipment and unforgiving of weakness. Our boat was purpose built, conceding nothing in the vital engineering and sailing functions. It was this confidence in the build that allowed us to depart so quickly, just three weeks after launching. The maiden passage to Greenland was her sea trial – she passed, with distinction – seven and a half days from Westport to Cape Farewell. The manner in which she handled the ice we met on Greenland's west coast gave us a lasting confidence.

Communications, by satellite phone and e-mail transmission – via radio link – are now becoming the norm and will soon be taken for granted. Unfortunately the downside of electronic communications aboard yachts is their vulnerability in a corrosive marine environment. Computers can, and will, crash just when you need them most. Luckily we had the expertise on board to revive computers and re-boot software.

Now *Northabout* lies in a snug berth near Westport, where construction is underway on the completion of the interior so rudely interrupted by its departure in 2001.

John Murray has made a film, 'In Franklin's Wake – The North West Passage' based on our adventure and is now completing another film, based on Gary's two seasons of shooting in the North East Passage.

There has been some recognition of this, the first-ever westward polar circumnavigation; awards and accolades have come our way and sometimes a pint!

Will we go back to the ice again? For me, the answer is, definitely not! We had good times in the north. But now my ambition is to do some relaxed cruising in home waters, enjoying life.

'But I shall go on. It is my plain duty.' Odysseus, Homer's wanderer

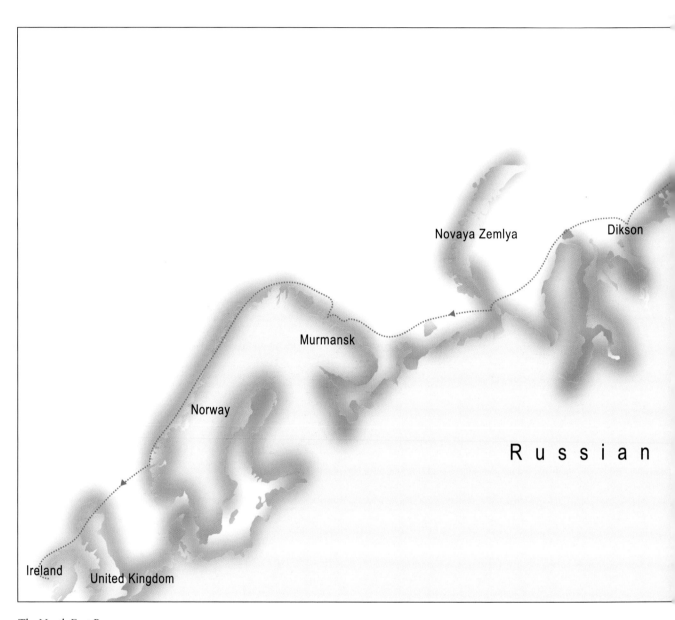

The North East Passage.

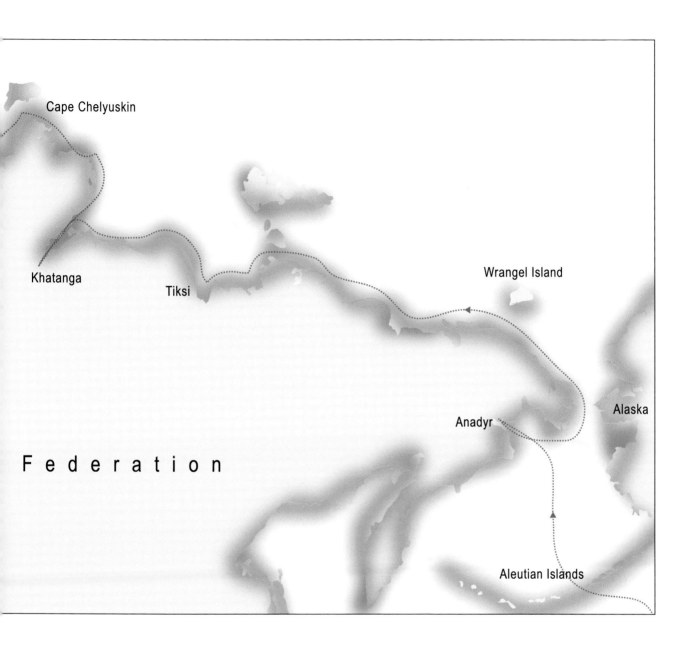

GLOSSARY
OF ICE TERMS

Ice is a constant presence throughout this book. This glossary may help.

Ice in the Sea

Ice in the sea is of direct concern to the polar traveller, because it restricts and sometimes controls his movements. It can also affect the propagation of radio waves, creating problems with radio transmissions. It can take the form of icebergs, growlers, brash ice, etc.

Icebergs

When a glacier flows into the sea, the buoyant forces of the water break off pieces from time to time and these pieces float away as icebergs. The principal danger from icebergs is their tendency to break and roll over, endangering any vessel in their vicinity. Icebergs generally have $^8/_{10}$ to $^9/_{10}$ of their mass below the water surface, therefore are more influenced by currents than by winds.

Growlers

A growler is a smaller piece of ice generally extending less than one metre above the sea surface but large enough to inflict serious damage to a vessel. Growlers get their name from the noise they make as they bob up and down in the sea.

Sea Ice

Sea ice is formed by the freezing of seawater and accounts for 95 per cent of all ice encountered.

Fast Ice

Fast ice is the term given to sea ice firmly attached to the coast or in shallow water (shoals).

Pack Ice

Pack Ice is the term used to describe any area of sea ice, other than fast ice. The pack can be described as *very open* (with an ice concentration of 1/10 to 3/10,) *open* (4/10 to 6/10,) *close* (7/10 to 8/10) and *compact* (10/10) with no water visible. *Northabout* could navigate through 1/10 to 3/10 ice cover. Ice-breakers are the only vessels that can navigate in 7/10 or heavier ice cover.

New Ice

A general term for newly-formed ice which includes frazil ice, grease ice, and slush.

Top: *Iceberg.* Above: *Growler.*

Top: *Grease ice forming pancake ice.* Above: *Brash ice.*

Pancake Ice

Pancake ice is composed of circular pieces of ice 30mm to 3 metres in diameter, up to 100mm thickness, with raised rims due to the pieces striking against one another. It may be formed on a slight swell from grease ice, slush or shuga.

First Year Ice

Sea ice of not more than one winter's growth, developing from young ice 300 mm to 2 metres thickness.

Second Year Ice

Second year ice is old ice which has survived one summer's melt.

Multi Year Ice

Old sea ice which has survived at least two summers' melt, also called 'Storis' in Greenland.

Frazil Ice

Represents the first stage of sea ice formation. Gives the sea an oily appearance.

Grease Ice

The next stage of freezing following the coagulation of frazil ice crystals to form a soupy layer.

Young Ice

Young ice, a transition stage between nilas and first year ice, may be classified as grey or grey-white. Grey may be 100 to 150 mm thick, grey-white may be 150 to 300 mm thick.

Brash Ice

Accumulations of floating ice made up of fragments not more than 2 metres across. Easily navigable.

Floe

A floe is any contiguous piece of sea ice, and is described in terms of several size catagories;

Small:	20 to 100 metres across
Medium:	100 to 500 metres across
Big:	500 to 2000 metres across
Vast:	2 to 10 km across
Giant:	over 10 km across.

Lead

A lead is an open area between ice floes. A lead between pack ice and shore is called a shore lead and one between pack and fast ice is a flaw lead. Navigation in these types of leads is dangerous, because if the pack ice closes with the fast ice, a ship can be caught between the two and driven aground or caught in the sheer zone between.

Ice Blink

A white reflection of sea ice on the clouds may give advance warning of ice field ahead.

GLOSSARY

A glossary of nautical terms for those who do not sail.

Abeam – at right angles to the keel of a vessel.

Aft – behind; towards the stern of a vessel.

Astern – behind; or towards the stern of a vessel.

Autopilot – an electric device, which automatically steers the vessel.

Ballast – weight carried low down in a vessel's bilge or keel to give her stability.

Bar – a shoal at the mouth of a river or harbour.

Beam – the extreme width of a vessel.

Berth – a sleeping place on board. Also a dock ashore.

Bilge – the space beneath the floor.

Bilge pump – a pump, electrically or engine driven, used to pump water from the bilges.

Boom – a horizontal spar at the foot of the mainsail.

Backstay – a wire rope supporting the mast leading aft.

Centreboard – a pivoting plate which can be lowered through a slot in the keel to provide lateral resistance and reduce leeway.

Clew – the lower aft corner of a sail.

Cockpit – a well near the stern from where a vessel is steered.

Close-hauled – sailing with the sails set for sailing towards the direction from which the wind is blowing. Sailing as close as possible into the wind.

Cutter rig – a fore-and-aft rigged vessel with one mast, a mainsail and two headsails.

Deviation – an error of the compass, caused by the proximity of ferrous metal.

Displacement – the weight of a vessel.

Draught – the depth of water required to float a vessel.

Following wind – wind blowing from astern.

Foot – the lower edge of a sail.

Fore – in front; the opposite to aft.

Forestay – a wire rope supporting the mast, leading from the masthead to the bow.

Frame – a rib of a vessel.

Freeboard – the height of a vessel's sides above water.

Gaff-rigged – a traditional sailing rig, with a quadrilateral mainsail supported by a gaff.

Goose winged – sails set when the wind is astern, usually two headsails set on opposite sides of the vessel.

Guardrail – a wire supported by stanchions, to prevent a person falling overboard.

Genoa – a large jib set on the forestay.

Grapnel – a small anchor with four arms for anchoring to ice floes.

Halyard – a line used to hoist sails.

Head – the bow, also the top corner of a sail.

Heads – the WC.

Heave-to – sails and helm are set in a manner that lets a sailing vessel look after itself in stormy seas. The vessel then lies almost stationary, in relative comfort.

Helm – the tiller or wheel used for steering.

Jib – a triangular sail set ahead of the mast, usually hoisted on the forestay.

Keel-cooled – *Northabout's* engine has a special keel-cooler. The engine cooling water is cooled in the keel in a closed circuit, which dissipates heat like a radiator in a car. Most other marine engines are cooled by constantly pumping seawater through them.

Lay-up – to berth a vessel for the winter.

Latitude – distance north or south of the equator, expressed in degrees and minutes.

Leech – the aftermost part of a sail.

Lee shore – a shore, downwind of a vessel. This can be a dangerous situation for a sailing vessel.

Leeway – the amount of sideways movement made through the water by a vessel; that is, the difference between the course steered and the course made good.

Lifeline – a line secured to a person as a safety precaution when working on deck or aloft.

Logbook – a book, which contains a record of a voyage.

Longitude – distance east or west of the meridian line of Greenwich, expressed in degrees and minutes.

Luff – the forward part of a sail.

Mainsail – a fore and aft sail, set on the aft side of the mast.

Mast – a long metal or timber pole standing upright in a vessel, supported by stays and shrouds, on which sails are set.

Masthead – the top of a mast.

Roller furling – a device, which reduces sail by rolling a sail around a stay.

Running rigging – sheets, topping lifts, halyards, etc. by which sails are controlled, as opposed to standing rigging, which is fixed.

Reef – to reduce the area of a sail, by tying or rolling up part of it.

Sheet – a rope used to control a sail, may be attached to its clew or a boom.

Spreaders – a metal strut on a mast to give the rigging more spread, also called a crosstree.

Standing rigging – shroud, stays, etc., which support the mast, and are not handled in the sailing of the vessel.

Staysail – a triangular fore and aft sail set on a stay.

Stay – a wire rope giving fore and aft support to a mast.

Stringer – a longitudinal strengthening member attached to the hull plating.

Stepped – raised the mast into position.

Stanchion – a support for guard-wire, etc.

Starboard – the right-hand side of a vessel facing forward.

Shroud – a wire rope giving athwartship support to a mast.

Sloop – a fore- and after-rigged vessel similar to a cutter but having one headsail instead of two.

Sea anchor – a parachute like device deployed in the sea to slow a vessel's drift in heavy weather.

Tiller – a wooden or metal bar attached to the rudder head by which the vessel is steered.

Trade-wind-rig – sailing with the wind astern with poled-out headsails set on opposite sides of the vessel.

Transducer – an electronic fitting in a vessels bottom, which sends echo signals to the bottom to measure depth.

Variation – the difference between true and magnetic north at any place.

Wind-vane self-steering – a device, which uses wind and waterpower to steer the vessel automatically.

Winch – a mechanical device consisting of a drum and crank arm, around which sheets are lead to increased pulling power.

Windlass – a type of winch for hauling anchor cable.

Moor – to make a vessel secure alongside a quay, etc.

Meridian – a true north-and-south line.

Port – the left-hand side of a vessel when looking forward.

Underway – a vessel is said to be underway when she is moving through water.

INDEX